46

# ESTRANGER

# RESCUE PRESS
## CHICAGO, CLEVELAND, IOWA CITY

Design by Sevy Perez
In Knockout HTF and Chronicle Text
rescuepress.co

# ESTRANGER

## ERIK

## ANDERSON

FOR MY PARENTS, FOR THEIR PARENTS

FOR MY SON

In his note on the text of *Estranger*, Erik Anderson refers to the *lively debates, recent and otherwise, around the ethics of fact and factitiousness.* Here the reader may recall the swath of conversation over the past couple decades about "creative nonfiction," the "lyric essay," fact-checking and the "lifespan of a fact" (as one prominent volume, by John D'Agata, was titled), authenticity, fake memoirs and real novels... *Lively* is a nicely wry adjective; *ferocious* would be another. With a similarly quiet playfulness, Anderson mentions these debates only to note that they have *no or very little place in these pages*—so, surely, it is not my place to give them one now. Yet this phrase delights me: to have no place in these pages. For of all the achievements of *Estranger*, the most remarkable is how this text creates an experience to which it barely refers: this work evokes an acute intellectual and emotional trial that does not seem to take place here, in these pages, but rather—powerfully—within their reader. *Its prime virtue was to point at what was no longer there*: this is Anderson's criticism of the replica of Thoreau's cabin that now awaits tourists at Walden Pond; but the line may be stolen to describe the strengths of his own work, this neither-memoir-nor-fiction. To represent his profound experience of estrangement, Anderson does not re-enact it—as a memoir might, surveying and mapping the past, finally determining its meaning—but enacts it anew, and in us: this book lends new reality to a reflection of what is no longer there.

I used the word *trial* deliberately. To say that our word *essay* comes from the French verb *to try* was once just etymology and is now workshop clunker. Anderson's contemporary approach to the essay inclines me toward a further neither-fake-nor-real wordplay: to try, as in, to place before the law. Anderson articulates the potential beauty of such judgment—to be seen, known, judged—almost offhand, as our narrator considers the empathy of his therapist: *that someone whose life. . .so little resembled his own might understand him this fully.* The horrors of such judgment—to be seen by another—we all know. And what if the one who fails to understand you, who will not resemble you, is yourself? The encounter with the self as stranger, the stranger as self that occurs in this book possesses the rigor and consequence and exposure of a trial: we feel how the stakes are this high. Yet it is precisely Anderson's approach to form that transcends the limitations of any discourse of psychology or of simple selfhood, of any one discourse, whether that of the memoir or novel, literary criticism or notebook, any of the genres through which *Estranger* moves. Anderson knows that no one form should take place here. His attentive movements render instead the spaces in between forms: what a trial can't determine, what a true story can't tell, what a novel falsifies. This book's motion—which feels as open as the landscapes in which *Estranger* is set, the journey through mountains and sky to the pre–ghost-town of Walden, Colorado, that our narrator pursues—reveals a marriage, new fatherhood, a family's history, and the ever-urgent question of the role of art in daily life, as grappled with by figures ranging from Hou Hsiao-Hsien, Werner Herzog, and Lao Tzu, to twenty-first–century poets losing their place in the neoliberalizing university.

*A part of me. . . felt some gaps in the record were better left in place*, Anderson writes, and this book is the record of those gaps, a place for what can never quite take place, a site where the self is neither familiar nor strange, neither you nor I. We are proud to invite you to share in *Estranger*, the third work in Rescue Press's Open Prose Series.

Hilary Plum
CO-EDITOR, OPEN PROSE SERIES
SPRING 2016

The first step in attending to our education is to observe the strangeness of our lives, our estrangement from ourselves, the lack of necessity in what we profess to be necessary. The second step is to grasp the true necessity of human strangeness as such, the opportunity of outwardness.

Stanley Cavell, *Senses of Walden*


"My father," he had said. It sounded so strange coming out of his mouth. It meant at the same time his father's father too, and his father before him, as if someone had accidentally struck a bell and all the other bells began to resonate with it, the bells that over the course of many generations had been cast from the same metal, all the way back to the beginning.

Hans Keilson, *Comedy in a Minor Key*

In early December of 2010, after an exhausting autumn, I filled an already brimming box with an assortment of loose ends and drove to a cabin on the Poudre River, west of Fort Collins, where I spent several weeks in a peculiar frame of mind, wrestling with certain notions of strangeness that had arisen in me not long after the birth of my son two years prior—notions which, by their fugitive nature, had resisted elaboration in my daily life. The place was a mobile home done up to look like a log cabin from the outside. It had been brought here on a flatbed truck, the manager told me as she confirmed my credit card. I was tempted to ask for a refund, but it was already late afternoon and, as so often was the case in those days, I didn't have the strength to explain, or maybe the heart to express, my objections. Weeks earlier, I had rented a log cabin over the internet, but where I was staying was a prefabricated version made primarily from plastic. The woman, Darcy, was friendly enough, and the cabin was situated in the canyon in such a way that I couldn't see the two-lane highway even if it was impossible not to hear it. She gave me the key, attached to a plastic log, and after I had driven my car a little way up the road, I placed my bag on an armchair, my box on the kitchen table, and lay down on the bed, where I promptly fell asleep.

It was dark when I awoke. I was hungry, but hardly in the mood to cook any of the food I had left in the car. I drove several miles downstream to the restaurant I had passed earlier that afternoon, and where that night, among the stuffed animal heads and antique shotguns mounted on the walls, I was struck by the contrast to other canyons I had spent time in—places where rock climbers, hikers, and skiers prevailed. When I mentioned this to the man working as bartender, waiter, and host, he said that here, too, the change had come, but business had also picked up, and he had even, on account of the Buddhist retreat center up the road, added several vegetarian options to the menu. For now, there were only a few other customers: a pair of rough-looking characters watching a football game at the bar and an ancient couple hunched over their plates in silence. I sat amid a small cluster of tables with a distant view of the river and, as I looked out at the trickle of water flowing through the snow, considered the bizarre, sometimes painful, reconciliations one negotiates, through language, with time.

Back in the cabin that night, I removed the contents of my box and set them on the table. On the outside I had written, months earlier, the word *STRANGENESS* in large block letters, and since then I had placed in it, one by one, the items it now contained. Laid out in front of me, I felt overwhelmed not so much by their quantity but by the intractable connections among them. Was there something dishonest about the whole endeavor, some element of disloyalty either to my family or myself? Would the individual elements bridge the gaps between me and those I loved, as I hoped, or would they be the wedges that only made those gaps larger? I took a photograph from the table and, a little buzzed from the beer I'd had with dinner, lay down on the checkered bedspread.

On TV Mark Zuckerberg was being interviewed about the recent hit film, based on a nonfiction bestseller, that portrayed his origins in an unflattering light. Why is it, I thought, that interviewers never ask the most interesting questions? My questions, anyway, were about the tricky business of a subject describing itself, about the distortions that result from the translation of a three-dimensional being into a two-dimensional profile—a process that has always reminded me of the artist Kara Walker's ghostly silhouettes, her charged figures that tend, deliberately, toward caricature. For me, the dilemma was related to exaggerated features and grotesque distortions that, as their purchase increased, threatened to replace the persons they had originally intended to represent. Walker's art was about the dangers of conflating the actual with the imaginary; Zuckerberg had made billions encouraging us to revel in that conflation.

As the inane interview continued, I looked more closely at the photograph I had brought into the bedroom. The year is 1955. My grandfather's left arm curls around my father's body while his right hand grabs the edge of the boat. My father's right arm rests along my grandfather's thigh. The person taking the photo is probably my great-grandfather, my grandmother's father; my grandmother and great-grandmother are somewhere on shore. The men float on one of the fifteen lakes that make up the Cisco Chain, straddling the border between northern Wisconsin and Michigan's upper peninsula. The nearest city is either Duluth or Green Bay, but the family has driven up from the south side of Chicago, where my grandfather works as a salesman for Wyler's. Neither smiles in the photo. Underneath his bright sun hat, the look in Dad's eyes is a mixture of fear and distrust, and though my grandfather's eyes are hidden behind a pair of dark aviators, he is clearly frowning. They wear the mantles of father and son awkwardly, as though the roles are foreign to them or imposed by an inherited sense of propriety. Then again, I may be reading too much into the photograph or reading it in light of the events that flowed from that moment. Either way, I can't help myself.

Of their serious expressions, Dad writes: it occurs to me the photographer would have had to say smile, thereby spooking every muskie, northern pike, and largemouth bass in a two-mile radius. My great-grandfather, he says, was one serious fisherman. He remembers the instructions: absolute silence. In the picture he is three years old, almost four. Maybe, as other photos from the trip suggest, he enjoyed fishing. Maybe the mood lightened once they got off the boat. His most vivid memory of the trip, however, is seeing the rocky bottom of the lake near the shoreline after he fell off the end of the dock, and though his letter describing the experience is funny, I wondered that night in the cabin about the connection between the hero's welcome he received when his mother, who dove into the water to rescue him, returned with him to the surface and the joke—told by his grandfather—that the fish stopped biting for the remainder of the day.

On TV, the conversation had turned to privacy, but as I watched Zuckerberg sit comfortably, unruffled by the questions, it occurred to me that the users had never been his customers, as I had always thought; they were, instead, products delivered to his real customers, the advertisers off of whom he had made his fortune. His business demanded that these products, the users, surrender their privacy at the login page. Under the rubric of community, he had duped us out of our identities. Our so-called networks were nothing more than vehicles for selling ad space. And yet he had also helped usher in an age when to be visible (particularly as an image) has become everything, an age in which a refusal to be seen is to some degree a refusal to exist. But then wasn't I, in coming to the cabin, refusing to be seen? Wasn't it this demurral, insomuch as it was about defending borders or choking back feeling, that I had recently found so exhausting? I wanted something more from myself, something more from Zuckerberg, too. I wanted the carefully constructed façade to crack, wanted to find a way to crack it. But I also wanted to know, watching him on the flat-screen TV, what he thought about the thing he had created, which, for better or worse, was not only a revolution in itself, but in the months to come would play a logistical role in the mass protests that would topple several Arab leaders. No advertisement had ever done anything remotely similar, but the drone of the interview and its interspersed commercials still put me to sleep, and although I must have woken up and turned off the TV at some point, in the morning the picture of my father was still in my hand.

The groceries had sat in the car overnight. Much of the food was frozen, and while I made coffee I set the loaf of bread out to thaw on the counter. I grabbed the photograph from where I had left it on the bedside table, which, I only then noticed, was bolted to the floor. The immobility of the furniture added to the sense that the entire place had been created out of whole cloth, molded from a single piece of material. It seemed a marvel of design, a marriage of matter and manufacturing.

I saw Darcy walking down the road with an old German shepherd. The dog limped a little. Bad hips, I thought, remembering how, as a kid, our own large dog, a golden retriever, had struggled to get around as she got older. As Darcy passed the cabin, she saw me in the window and waved. I guessed that she was about my mother's age, but I imagined people often mistook her, like my mother, for a much younger woman. After she moved beyond the window's frame, I began to write, but now, as I look over my notes from that morning, I can't so much see the arc of my thinking as the intuition of that arc, which, to my tremendous irritation, continued for years to defy my attempts to define it. I see myself struggling, in other words, with what I can now say freely.

One's father is the first stranger one meets. This is no less true with my son than it is with my father. The mother may be the primal site and source, but the father will never be a site precisely. Instead, he is the first non-site, and that initial distance, though it may narrow over time, will never collapse into the intimacy experienced by a mother and child, in which another body can mean home. The world itself is at its strangest—we are most estranged from the world—when we first enter it. I don't see comfort or fascination in the eyes of newborns, but rather bewilderment, as though no vocabulary is adequate to the encounter. Then again, newborns can only see as far as the distance between their mother's nipples and her face, so maybe what I interpret in their expressions as estrangement is simply limited eyesight.

Some have claimed to see in newborns a profound recognition of the cosmic joke that's just been played on them; for my part, I'm fairly certain that in spite of the crying they don't know sadness any more than they know humor, although we immediately bombard them with both. Early on in his life, for instance, "Somewhere Over the Rainbow" made its way into the rotation of lullabies I sang to our son. These were a mixture of standards, pop songs, and the children's lyrics that, having forgotten them long ago, I picked up from my wife, whose memory for music is remarkably good. Because of its association with *The Wizard of Oz* I had always assumed it was a happy song, but the fact that it celebrates a place that only exists in lullabies—somewhere *over the rainbow* where (unlike here) the sky is blue, birds fly, and dreams come true—is a bleak reflection of the singer's condition. Even the longing for escape is distant: *someday*, I repeated twice daily for the better part of a year, *I'll wish upon a star*, but not today.

Don't worry, one friend assured me early on, there's nothing you can do to not fuck up your kids. All you can do is mitigate the effects. I remembered the famous line from Wordsworth, the child is the father of the man, and I had it in my head almost immediately to write something not only about the strangeness I felt in parenting a son but also this reverse parentage wherein the child forces the adult to grow up. But what I first noticed about being a father—and this is what preoccupied me that morning in the cabin—had little to do with the strangeness I anticipated. Instead, I felt time dissolving. Days did not begin, did not end. The past prefigured a future, repeated. Time both moved and stood still, and caught there in the middle of that tension I was singularly disordered. Patterns that had revolved around the earth's rotation found in our son a new axis. Sleeplessness deranges the senses, but more unsettling was the disruption of the singleness of purpose that, like the circadian model, I had taken for granted. For years I had existed mainly for myself, but now there was this joyful little person in the room, eliciting my delirious allegiance. Normalcy eventually returned, but, as when a meteor strikes, its character had been forever altered. I returned to work but as another person, a stranger, one who spoke in another alphabet, a mixture of coo and cry.

As I finished a second cup of coffee, eyes alternating between the picture and the notebook, I had the sudden fear that I would never understand my son and he would never understand me. I hoped for tenderness. I hoped for solicitude. I hoped for long conversations by a fireside that, as I closed the notebook and began to put on my boots, I could not yet imagine but dimly perceived, somewhere there beyond the threshold of the present, out past the foreseeable future, when my son's life had taken its own, independent shape. Maybe fatherhood itself is a crisis, I thought, demanding emotions I'd learned to refuse. Outside, the morning sun was casting long shadows through the rocky canyon, and down the road I saw Darcy carrying firewood into her house. The German shepherd was still there, waiting on the porch. I was afraid as I walked around the car, scraping off the windows— afraid of a child who hadn't yet had the opportunity to resent me, afraid of distances that threatened to expand. Mostly I realized, as I climbed into the car, that I had been too absorbed in my thoughts to make breakfast. The loaf of bread was still thawing on the counter, and my stomach was now grumbling.

I set Thoreau's *Journal* on the passenger seat and began the hour drive over the mountains into the long, wide basin home to the town of Walden, Colorado. I had seen the name on maps for years, and though I didn't expect much of Thoreau to show up, I was disappointed to learn first that the town's small museum, housed in an old cabin far more authentic than my own, was closed on Mondays, and then later, from an elderly waitress who had the peculiar habit of scratching her ear with a pencil as she spoke, that the place had been named after a postmaster. It is essential that a man confine himself to pursuits, I read, which lie next to and conduce to his life, which do not go against the grain, either of his will or his imagination. The scholar finds in his experience some studies to be most fertile and radiant with light, others dry, barren, and dark. If he is wise, he will not persevere in the last, as a plant in a cellar will strive toward the light. He will confine the observations of his mind as closely as possible to the experience of his senses. His thought must live with and be inspired with the life of the body. Some men, Thoreau continues, endeavor to live a constrained life, to subject their whole lives to their wills, as he who said he would give a sign if he were conscious after his head was cut off—but he gave no sign.

In the restaurant I ate an omelet so out of proportion with my needs that even when I cut it in half I could barely finish it. I stared out into the mostly vacant dining room, the size and décor of which conformed perfectly to the meal I had attempted to finish. At the front counter I paid the waitress, whose pencil again touched the top of her left lobe as she swiped my credit card, and after walking the broad, treeless streets for an hour I found a liquor store and bought some supplies. Where was the channel where my own life flowed? Was I like that plant in the cellar, striving toward the light? I gathered there wasn't much to see in Walden except the sky, so endless as to inspire something like dread. The surrounding space felt impenetrable to me, and, just as I had on trips to the San Luis Valley or to southern Park County, I came away stripped of something. Perhaps it's my sense of irony that I lose in these unequivocal spaces. Or perhaps it's my sense of self that's dismantled, which would be entirely in keeping with the sinking feeling that overcame me as I carried my purchases to the car and drove, with my defeated Thoreau, back up the mountain.


I spent that afternoon reading and, my notebook attests, obsessing over a distinct memory of sitting on my grandfather's lap in a pink armchair my grandmother later had reupholstered. The more deeply I considered the memory, the less it felt like my own. Maybe it was a lingering effect of the trip to Walden, but I felt as though, contrary to reality, I were seeing the memory from the outside, as though a third party had entered my body and was now sitting in the living room of my grandparents' immaculate home in suburban Chicago, as though it had been his grandfather who, his father had once told him, expected nothing less than perfection, his grandfather who used to follow his grandmother around to check up on her work, making sure the beds were made to spec, the toilets properly scrubbed, that the floors revealed no more wax than necessary.

That final Christmas his—I mean *my*—grandfather was alive, the source of my memory, my father confronted him. He had overheard him saying to my grandmother something along the lines of *can you believe our son is in there bathing the boys?* I remember those baths and the story time that followed, how my father fell asleep over Laura Ingalls Wilder. These rituals that, for me, have always been hallmarks of my father's care were something else in my grandfather's eyes, a sign of weakness, maybe, or of softness. I suppose it was a generational clash that night in Chicago, as one model of parenthood replaced another.

Dad had told me, on a recent visit, that he wasn't sure whether he should have taken his father to task, but that it can be tough to find your voice with your parents. To get them to accept you as you are. This was a Monday, I remember. We were having Chinese. My son, around seven months old at the time, must have been sleeping in the other room. There was wine and laughter, but after my parents had flown home to Michigan and I was cleaning, I found on the cat's bed a photo of my father taken one Christmas several years ago. The picture, in which he holds a power drill to his head like a gun, was tucked into a printout of the photo of him fishing with his father. Did he see these photos, I wondered? When he couldn't find and went looking for our tabby cat, George?

Nearby on the floor, pilfered from my parents' bookshelves, was my father's copy of the 1965 *Boy Scout Handbook*, printed the year he turned fourteen. The Norman Rockwell cover shows a decked-out scout carrying this very edition of the *Boy Scout Handbook* with himself on the cover, which means that on the cover of that cover is a smaller version of the *Boy Scout Handbook* on which an even smaller scout is carrying an even smaller handbook. In the background and to the right, one scout pitches a tent while two others make a fire; to the left, several others appear to be hiking along a stream. Just inside the cover on the first page, my father's name is written in his adolescent hand. In my notebook, I wrote about the curly flourishes in the capital *S* and *A* of his signature, curving down to the left and then back up to the right. But I was also intrigued by the text to the left of the Be Prepared insignia at the bottom of the page, which explains that the 1965 printing includes *A change in the treatment for snake bite—pages 311–13*. I turned to page 311, but without the 1964 printing to refer to, I had no idea what the change might have been. Both poisonous and nonpoisonous snakes are apt to strike when cornered, it says, and fainting may occur because of the emotional upset. I had a hard time imagining my father getting bitten by a snake, let alone fainting from such a bite, but I also recorded that when we walked together down to a nearby lake on that visit we saw a large spider on the sidewalk. My father nudged it gently with his foot, and it assumed what must have been its most intimidating pose: one of its eight legs cocked up, as though to strike. I had included the *Handbook* in my box of strangeness, and in the cabin I noted my curiosity as to what it had to say about spider bites but found no entry for spider in the index. So instead I flipped to the opening section, *YOU—AMERICAN BOY*, and copied down the following:

> Have you ever dreamed of hiking the wilderness trails that were worn down under moccasins hundreds of years ago? Do you hear in your imagination the almost soundless dip-dip of Indian canoe paddles or the ring of the axe of an early pioneer hewing a home out of the American wilderness? Have you followed with your mind's eye the covered wagons on the trek across the continent? Have you thought of the men and women who built our country by their determination and devotion?
>
> You are the descendent of those people. You are the guardian of what they built. You are the American on whom the future of our wonderful country depends.

I'm not certain what significance I saw in this passage, or in the sentences I found on the following page: *Today you are an American boy. Before long you will be an American man.* I suspect it had to do, on one hand, with the difficulty of finding one's voice, as my father had put it, and on the other, with the pernicious ways in which such a voice can be adopted, inherited, or imposed. The hokey, romantic prose of the *Handbook* propagated certain myths about our descent and suppressed versions that ran counter to them; in the inimitable practicality of the 1960s Boy Scouts, I didn't see a willingness to confront what happened to the *dip-dip* of those paddles, but the grandfather I would never know lurked in the shadows of those sentences, a kind of double, and I suspected that his story—if only I could learn it—might elucidate my own.

I worked deep into the night and awoke late the next morning. Watching fresh snow fall through the kitchen window, I thought of the big basement window at home, on the other side of which a metal ladder led to ground level and where for an hour each morning my reflection hunched over the computer's. Often as I wrote I tricked myself into thinking the ladder did not lead to the courtyard but instead continued infinitely toward the light. Soon enough I would hear my son waking up several floors above me. He has always been an early riser and in those days shouted about firemen, garbage trucks, or the hippopotamus we saw *taking a bath* at the zoo. He would begin jumping up and down in his crib, and the squeaks from its frame would filter down through the air ducts. It annoyed me at the time, but I also remembered thinking *don't react.* I have often struggled to embrace his outsized presence in my life, but now—and this was the question I set myself that morning after my trip to Walden—how to do this in writing? The springs of words may squeak, but could I make them do it on cue?

I opened another dog-eared book from my box, Werner Herzog's *Conquest of the Useless,* and began to read in the lonely armchair tucked between the kitchen and the door. Although it had a lamp and end table beside it, both bolted down, of course, it was ideally situated not so much for reading as for putting on and taking off one's shoes. Through the windows, I saw the snow blowing more fiercely, and after a while there was a knock at the door. I felt a blast of frozen air as Darcy stepped in out of the cold, kicking the snow off her boots on the door jamb. Had I heard about the storm? Several feet were possible, and she wanted to make certain I had everything I needed. I pushed the mess on the kitchen table to one side and offered her some coffee. We sat. She told me that the cabin belonged to a retired dentist in the Fort, as she called it. As with most of the cabins she managed, he was only up there a few times a year, for fishing and hunting trips with his family. She owned four places in the area, all built by her husband, who had come up with the idea for the business shortly before he had, without warning, left her to raise their two teenage boys on her own. Kids grow up, she said, thank god. One was studying in Boulder, the other in Greeley. They would be home for the holidays the following week.

But what was my story? What was I doing up here all alone? I told her about my son, and about what I called my work on strangeness. I was used to people's eyes glazing over, but Darcy's probed, and as they did I began to see the outlines of a younger self. Surely I had read Camus's *The Stranger*, she asked, and when I said it had been nearly twenty years, she offered to loan me her copy. And what's this got to do with it, she asked, pointing to the Herzog. I flipped to an entry dated August 4, 1980, where Herzog writes that a failure to embrace his dreams would be a disgrace so great that sin itself could not find a name for it. At the time, I said, Herzog was working on a film deep in the Peruvian jungle, where the burden of his particular dream—a large steamship climbing a steep hill—had encountered some extraordinary obstacles. Locations had fallen through, actors had quit, funding had nearly collapsed, and the indigenous Peruvians on whose labor the production depended were rebelling. I explained that the main character in the film, an opera aficionado and would-be rubber baron, is a veiled version of Herzog himself. Like the director, he has a dream that defies realization: to build a grand opera house in the jungle, where his idol, Enrico Caruso, might perform. What appears to be Fitzcarraldo's folly is Herzog's too: neither is willing to accede to the demands of reality. In this way, they are like the natives they meet in the jungle, about whom one character, a missionary, says, we simply cannot cure them of their idea that ordinary life is only an illusion, behind which lies the reality of dreams. Darcy was nodding, so I added, looking over the spilled contents of my box, as though they might constitute another sort of hill, that for most of us the opposite is true: a truth is not a truth until it lies on the dissecting table, systematically pulled to pieces by a diligent technician.

But dragging a ship over a mountain is madness, she said. I took a sip of my coffee, and for a moment there was only the snow's silence. The Brazilian engineer Herzog hired to lift the ship over the mountain, I said finally, recommended leveling it to a 12-percent grade. But Herzog wouldn't allow that. They would lose the central metaphor of the film. Metaphor for what, she asked, but I thought that even Herzog didn't know. Maybe it's just an image slumbering in all of us, Herzog had told the engineer, and he just happened to be the one to introduce him, the engineer, to a brother he had never met, so to speak. I suppose it's true, she said, that the more we analyze a dream, the more mundane it becomes. But how to trust a dream, I asked. How to trust a metaphor that promises to carry us nowhere?

So what does this have to do with strangeness, she asked. What does this have to do with your family? The obvious answer, I said, is that I'm here to figure it out, but on some level I don't really want to know. That's the problem with following your nose, she said, you don't always like where it leads. She smiled and tipped back her mug, holding it in the air for a second as she turned to look out the window. After a little sigh, she set her coffee back down. I didn't always live up here, you know. In the seventies, she told me, land was cheap and her husband's parents bought up a bunch of it, both in the Fort, where they still lived, and here in the mountains. The idea was to sell some of it to them eventually, but after her husband John left her with the boys, they just signed it over to her outright. John had always been something of a brooder, she went on, and his parents never quite knew what to do with him. When he brought her home from college one summer, an outgoing girl from Long Island, they were shocked. She couldn't exactly explain it either, but there was something rugged and otherworldly about him. He wasn't like other guys she knew, all sports and beer.

He talked about the *Bhagavad Gita* and knew the names of plants. She didn't know what to expect when they got married, she said, and adding kids to the mix only confused whatever expectations she had.

John was handy like his father, and even though he'd gone to school to be something else—he'd been pre-law—he wound up working construction. He kept talking about the land, how he wanted to move up here with the boys and raise them to be strong as bears. So they did. He built a little two-room hut down the way, and the four of them spent the winter of 1990 in it. The boys were barely out of diapers. It took him two summers to build that house, but over the following years, he built, sometimes with his father's help, several others. She didn't love it up here, but the boys were happy and, because of the housing boom, John had plenty of work in the mountains and down in the Fort. She guessed the marriage got lost in it all, and when he left she couldn't say she really missed him. He had worked long days for years, and on the weekends he would chip away at his projects or take the boys fishing.

We were nearly done with our coffee when she added that she had once thought she might be a writer herself. She had majored in English, and had even started a graduate program at Colorado State, but the older she got the less she felt any need to add to the torrent of language in the world. Besides, she said, my life's been a boring one, full of babies and books. I'm not complaining, but I sometimes wonder what might have happened if I hadn't met John, who I might have become. It's never too late, I said, but she shook her head and told me that was the great myth of youth. At her age she knew it was too late for some things. It was a sensation she was becoming more familiar with over time. She felt much of her life was inaccessible to her now, and she warned me it was a process that only accelerated with age. I am torn, she said, between not wanting to remember much of what's happened in the past fifty years and being unable to forget certain scenes. Still, it isn't so much that pleasant or unpleasant memories fade but that others rise unpredictably from the shadows and then you spend whole weeks chasing them down the hallways, like mice you just can't get rid of.

There was another silence, the two of us looking out at the snow, before she abruptly stood, placed her mug in the sink, and stepped toward the door. You shouldn't be here, she said then, firmly but kindly. It was a mother's scolding, tempered with affection. She brought an old woolen cap out from her pocket and, as she moved to open the door, pulled it over her closely cropped salt-and-pepper hair. Whatever it is you're looking for, she said, turning back to me once more, you're not going to find it, not here.

The heaps of snow predicted that day never materialized, and though there were flurries throughout the morning and well into the afternoon, by evening the stars had come out and I drove to the restaurant, where Jim, the waiter, bartender, and host, was washing some glasses behind the bar. There were a few more customers this time, and a woman I gathered was Jim's wife was attending to them. I slowly picked at greasy fries, drowning them in ketchup, and imagined the life that might have been for Darcy, the lives, perhaps irretrievable now, that might have been for me. Much as I hated to admit it, much as I sympathized with the abandoned wife and kids, I understood John's desire to leave. Even if it condemned his wife to a kind of imprisonment, he had pursued his freedom, having been seduced by its allure. Maybe it was this Darcy had seen in me.

I was reminded, sitting alone in the restaurant, of the short trip I had taken several weeks earlier to Los Angeles to promote my first book. There had been '30s movie scores streaming through hidden speakers in the airport, and throughout LA I had also spotted the ubiquitous Route 66 signs everywhere from the Santa Monica pier to a barbecue joint in Koreatown. I thought about the fiction of Los Angeles that paraded as its history, and I wondered, on bus rides across the city that lasted hours, whether LA's true history—including the Watts riots of 1966 and the more widespread ones of 1992—had become, in popular memory, a fiction. It struck me that the hidden LA must be the truer one, and that the visible one was a fake. Fiction may be a setting contiguous to reality, I wrote that night, but if nonfiction more properly corresponds to the truth, then reality is defined by what it isn't. The real takes shape through what's next to it, much as Darcy's life, or my wife's for that matter, was set in relief by her husband's illusions. To arrive at the real, then, perhaps you must first define unreality. Falsehood may not be contingent on truth but truth on falsehood.

Scanning those lines a month later, however, much deeper into the depression those weeks in the cabin had aggravated, I read *falsehood* as *fatherhood*, and at once I could see how it all connected, how my young son, with his endless emotional needs and my inability to address them, had brought about the crisis, which both was and was not about him, as it was and was not about my father, or his father, or LA, or Zuckerberg, or Darcy, or Herzog. All of us were guilty, but for that reason none of us were. Estrangement was just our condition, or our conditioning, and the challenge, I realized, my challenge, would be to treat it as a starting point, not a destination.

That night, after the lights down the road in Darcy's house had gone out, I considered how my son, long asleep by then, intuitively knew, outside of his dreams, that an upturned chair could be a steamroller, that a spoon could be a firetruck, that even a dinosaur could be rescued from a burning building—and all of it without any irritable reaching after fact and reason. Seen in this light, the arc of childhood may be a sad, slow drift toward the normative. I might have laughed the week prior when he ran around in circles saying he was a robot cowboy, but in my head I knew there was no such thing. As a parent, I so often found myself saying this is cute, this is crazy, this is not what you do with a fork. But part of what makes a child's life so enviable is how porous those boundaries are. Whereas adults abide in what has sometimes seemed to me a walking rigor mortis, children shift and seep. I tried that night, as I have tried since, to see the world through my son's eyes, but this is like seining for plankton. I imagine what it's like to see a live elephant for the first time. A hippopotamus wallowing in a pool or a tapir tracing slow circles in his enclosure. But this is difficult work. I can't seem to break through my mold.

## 2

That winter, he began seeing Rahim in a windowless room on the fifth floor of a building notable for the shiny rows of abandoned fitness machines visible from the street. He had tried to defuse the awkwardness of their initial encounter by observing that the gym was apparently failing, to which Rahim had responded, on the first of those Tuesday afternoons, that he sympathized with the eager attendants who smiled at him as he walked through the lobby, but that he couldn't bring himself to exercise in the building where he worked. And what about him, Rahim asked, making conversation, did he belong to a gym? He had always been suspicious of the gleaming machines, he said, which seemed to divide the body from its functions, or rather to divide the body into its functions, separating the physical act of running or lifting from any actual running or lifting. He preferred jogging, he said, as it was just him and the road, without mediation, although he only did it begrudgingly, more as a concession to his slowing metabolism and sedentary life than anything else. It was at that point that Rahim began to take notes and the pretense of the nonclinical encounter faded away.

He had been essentially assigned to the large practice by his wife's insurance company, and as he stared at the framed landscape on the wall where a window might have been, he wondered whether he should have been a more discerning consumer of mental health services. Even with sick people the market prevailed, and he considered that at least Rahim's furniture was new, though also cheap and inoffensive, like everything in the office. It was to his mind a damning statement about the culture that there were such profits, windfalls really, to be made off illness and death, but on the other hand, Rahim, who must have been only a few years older, hardly looked wealthy and his office was spartan at best. There was no couch, and the chair he sat in—a metal frame with an upholstered seat—might just as easily have found a home in an underfunded health clinic. He had immediately registered the small gay pride flag inserted into the potted jade plant on Rahim's bookshelf, the framed photograph on Rahim's desk that showed him standing with a tall, thin white man in his forties and what had to be the man's adolescent son, a scrawny kid whose fine features—sharp nose, deep eyes, high cheeks—were mirror images of the older man's.

Rahim had caught him glancing at the photo and explained. This was Bill, he said, and Bill's son Tony, and initially he left it at that. It came out slowly over the following months that Rahim and Bill were raising Tony together, against his mother's wishes, and that they found the United States, and Colorado in particular, an unwelcoming place for such an arrangement. Compounded by the fact that Rahim was a person of color, that he had been raised a Muslim first in southern Pakistan then in northern London, this country had never been an easy place for him, he would say much later, and he and Bill were considering emigrating to Vancouver, where Rahim had a supportive aunt and uncle.

There hadn't been a single event, he told Rahim when asked, that precipitated the call to the insurance company. Things had snowballed, he said, and Rahim pressed him to elaborate. He had taken to locking himself in his office, spending hours lying there on the white shag rug, staring at the ceiling. His wife claimed he often walked around the house in a daze, as though under the influence of some powerful sedative. Other times, after deep silences, he would explode in anger, yelling at her for cooking crunchy rice or screaming at their son for spilling his juice. His wife said the tension in the house was exhausting, and she wondered if he was entirely in his right mind, as he seemed, to her, to be losing his grip. And when did *he* notice something was wrong, Rahim asked. His wife had told him to leave, he said, just for a couple weeks that past December. He needed some time to get his head straight, she said, and she needed to figure out how she felt. He had spent two weeks in a cabin, where he had tunneled so deeply into himself that he had since struggled to get out. When he returned home, just before Christmas, his wife felt that he still wasn't there, that he hadn't been for some time. His distance was just too frustrating, and she demanded he start therapy, said the marriage depended on it. She hadn't asked for a divorce, he told Rahim, not yet, anyway, but the threat had rested uncomfortably between them ever since.

And what exactly had he been doing there in the cabin, Rahim asked, what had he been working on? He thought for a second and then—a little pretentiously, he felt, even as he was saying it—he quoted Julio Cortázar, who writes of a sudden estrangement, a *displacement* that alters the normal pattern of consciousness. He said that there are times when we cease to be ourselves and our circumstances, when we want to be both ourselves and something unexpected, ourselves and the moment when the door, which before and after opens onto the hallway, opens slowly to show the field where a unicorn sings.

When, predictably, this didn't clarify matters, when Rahim again encouraged him to elaborate, he said that the self who writes is not the self of the writer. Writing removes the writer, even as it repeats him: the words take shape on the page, and he transforms from the version of himself he assumes when running errands or scowling at the barking dog tethered outside the window. Something links the two, but that's another matter. A matter of what? Rahim asked. But this time he found himself gazing at the framed landscape on the wall, unable to answer. It was a view from the top of a small hill, looking across a meadow. Tall trees framed the scene, encircling the grass in the background. The page is an umbilicus, he offered, immediately regretting the analogy. He suspected Rahim would only push him further, make him tease out the identities on either side of that cord, the processes by which one accessed, while becoming inaccessible to, the other. It might be better to say, he quickly added, hoping to avoid any follow-up, that through writing the writer does not so much become a stranger to himself as he creates a place to live in language. His wife had been unmoved by the project, however, and he had since privately contented himself with the idea that displacement is the fantasy, or ecstasy, of writing.

Rahim suggested that he had still not responded to the question, that he had constructed an elaborate defense without it ever becoming clear what exactly he was defending, what set of values he was advancing or refuting. In quoting Cortázar, he had even called on an expert witness, but when had his life, much less his writing, turned into a trial? The defense was eloquent, Rahim said, even inspiring, but why was it necessary?

That winter, he was teaching night classes at a bargain-basement college in Denver, and on the days he taught he would drop his son off at the preschool behind his wife's office, which, because it was staffed by vegan women in long hemp skirts, he called hippie daycare. On the days he wasn't meeting with Rahim, he went straight to the office he shared with three other adjuncts, a tiny, windowless closet in a long row of tiny, windowless closets. He started teaching at 4:00 and finished at 10:00, with a short break between his second and third classes for dinner and the very occasional meeting with a student. For his labors, he received just over $9,000 a semester. There were no benefits.

His students were mostly misfits or misfires, overgrown children who were trying to be students or their older counterparts who had already failed at being a few things in their lives. Though he obviously didn't blame them for trying, there were often obstacles in his students' lives that made the successful completion of an essay writing course, let alone a full college education, particularly challenging. There were Iraq War vets clearly in thrall to their traumas, single mothers whose multiple children were spending the night at a favorite aunt's, and fuckups who had flunked out of one the state's better schools. For almost all of his students, his classes were additions to already full lives—jobs, families, or, in some cases, the limitations of parole. One of the other adjuncts he met in the copy room had told him the story of a student who had physically threatened her around midterms the year before. The student was kicked out of classes, but the campus police had escorted her to her car for the rest of the semester.

He quite liked the students, though he accepted as a matter of course that, in terms of their education, many were lost causes, and he was only bothered to see something of these foregone conclusions in the colleagues with whom he shared his cramped office, the highly fallible copy machine, and the overstuffed refrigerator. If working with the students inspired, at least some of the time, an overblown sense of justice, whiffs of desperation or resignation lingered after the other adjuncts as they passed through the hallway. They were a motley, haggard bunch, for some of whom their three classes here—the maximum the college would allow an adjunct to teach—were only part of a much larger wage slavery that spanned English departments across the city and beyond. He often worried about fully becoming one of them. He didn't want to give up on his hopes for less precarious, more remunerative work, and he didn't want to give in to an economic model in which his teaching amounted to disposable labor. But he was increasingly convinced that there were few alternatives. This was the shabby best, he thought, his overeducated life would get.

On his second visit to the tall building with the abandoned elliptical trainers, he told Rahim about the heavy bronze plaque from his paternal grandfather's gravestone he had discovered that Christmas in his parents' garage. His grandmother had recently arranged for the remains to be disinterred and transferred, at considerable expense, to the Michigan cemetery in which her second husband was also buried. The old marker now sat next to a collection of balls, bats, and other relics from his childhood. *Born November 10, 1928*, it read. *Died April 30, 1984*. Until that point, he had only a vague idea of how old his grandfather had been when he died, nor had he known his birthday or the date of his death.

But this was in keeping with how little he had been told about his grandfather. When, for instance, he had recently asked his grandmother about him in an email, she had responded that during World War II her family saved tin foil and sold it to the butcher (though she couldn't say why), that they added an orange tablet to the oleo to make it look like butter, and that as a child she was afraid the Gestapo would come to get her. She described being left alone as an infant for so long in her crib she began to peel the wallpaper. Her father hauled steel in a red semi, she wrote, seeming not to have registered the original question. Once his load shifted and he was lucky to have been thrown from the truck since had he been wearing his seat belt, or so he claimed, the steel coming through the cab would have killed him. She wrote that her mother's parents (the Limings) lived in Decatur, Illinois, and her father's parents on a farm somewhere in Michigan. She remembered having to pump the water and use an outhouse, and that they owned two horses, May and June. As poor as they were, she wrote, they always had enough to cook up a feast on their old wood stove, with their dog Spot keeping close in the winter.

She added, almost as a footnote, that she had married his grandfather on June 4, 1949, in Grace Evangelical Church on the south side of Chicago, right around the corner from her childhood home at 5919 South Albany. He had been stationed in Japan after the war, from roughly 1946 to 1948, and after they were married they moved to Rock Island, where he studied business at Augustana College and she worked as a secretary for a man named Will Power (his real name, she emphasized). His grandfather cleaned the incinerator to keep the rent low and sold Fuller brushes on the side.

He recounted the letter to Rahim, touching on the highlights, noting how remarkable it was for its silences. But what, Rahim asked, would knowing more achieve? What problems would it solve? He wanted to link his story to a larger one, he said, find some meaning in continuity. He had asked his father, after receiving her letter, whether his grandparents' story didn't embody a certain postwar cliché: the young soldier, home from the war, marries his sweetheart. They move to the suburbs, raise their children. They appear to be living out their version of the American Dream. But all the while cracks are developing. His father responded that, yes, he agreed, but that it was also their story and unquestionably more profound as they lived it. Much of this was settled history from his father's perspective, and for him, at sixty, there were few questions left to ask. Near the end of his life, his grandfather had threatened suicide many times. His grandmother had filed for divorce and his grandfather had lost his job. He'd felt his life was falling apart. There had been girlfriends and apartments on South Shore Drive—first the high life, then weekends with the kids—but all that was over now. And it left him feeling vulnerable, which had always made him aggressive. Something happened to make him believe he couldn't rely on others, his father said, and he had always viewed his grandfather's suicide as a desperate and defiant final statement.

But statement, Rahim wondered, of what? It seems to me there's something you're not saying, something you maybe can't bring yourself to say. Your attempt to understand ignores the fact that it's you who's trying to understand. Rahim leaned forward, resting his elbows on his thighs. Whose story are you telling?

During the first week of classes, a squirrelly student in a black leather jacket spoke at some length, unrelated to their discussion on the proper use of a semicolon, about the way fairy tales are always an argument for one worldview or another. The student's thinking was eccentric and elliptical, and he could see annoyance in the eyes of the other class members, even those who seemed to be deeply, chronically stoned. It wouldn't have been so bad, but each time he tried to cut the student off, the young man not only kept speaking but spoke louder, to the point where he was almost shouting, more assertively arguing the point none of them could follow. This is a crazy person, he thought. I am listening to a crazy person. After the student finally sputtered out, he returned to the acceptable linkages between independent clauses, astounded at how few of them were familiar with the term. The student stewed in the back row for the rest of the session, and when the group dispersed the student confronted him: why hadn't he allowed the class to discuss his ideas? He wasn't one of the worthless duds, the student said. In fact, he didn't even need this class—he had passed out of it. But the student also wasn't ruling out the possibility that things might get ugly, and though he wasn't quite sure what the student meant by that, a chill ran through him nonetheless.

Back in his closet of an office, in the short interval between his first two classes, he sent himself an email describing the exchange, worried that the young man was more a weasel than a squirrel, and though he fit the profile of a school shooter perfectly—awkward, lonely, middle class, and white—he kept his email factual, speculating only that the note's very existence suggested that he might need to call on it later. He had a premonition that the student, whose name resembled his own, would become a thorn in his side, necessitating all sorts of appeals to campus authorities he hadn't met. As he hurried to his next class across the sprawling institution—it had displaced a thriving Latino neighborhood when constructed, eliminating nearly all remnants of the previous architecture, save for a few churches—he imagined himself walking the route, a month or two hence, with a campus police officer at his side.

At the end of his second session with Rahim, he had dismissed the suggestion that he might be well-served by a selective serotonin reuptake inhibitor. He believed, he said, in his ability to manage his symptoms, or rather his emotions, through strength of mind. He found himself, however, having to repeat his refusal at the end of their third session, and at the beginning of their fourth. It worried him, Rahim's persistence, at least in part because he had wanted to see their sessions as an isolated intervention, necessary maintenance after which life would return to normal. Whereas he thought they were addressing a temporary problem, Rahim's treatment plan, whatever it was, seemed to call for long-term solutions.

It may have been because he refused medication that he had, on the other hand, accepted Rahim's request to record their sessions on video. He resisted this, too, at first, but Rahim had assured him the files were quite secure and would be reviewed only by him in preparation for future sessions. If and when treatment was ever discontinued, the files would be permanently deleted. And so he slowly became accustomed to the tiny black eyeball of a camera, inconspicuous enough that it blended in with the other items on Rahim's desk: the mug full of pencils and pens and highlighters, the box of tissues, the small stack of unused legal pads. It was a tidy desk, a tidy room. All of it purposefully anodyne, right down to the tan paint applied to the walls. If the room was offensive at all, it was in its inoffensiveness, to which the tiny camera merely contributed. Perhaps the greatest sin of contemporary life, he thought, was its excess of so-called good taste, the degree to which everyone was playing it safe, buying homes and filling them with new appliances, covering the walls with neutral colors. Why was it that people never painted their dining rooms black, their bathrooms hot pink, but settled instead for colors with names like *cumulus* and *grey goose*?

Much as he found himself ill at ease in many tastefully appointed homes, he may have gotten used to the camera but was never quite comfortable in its gaze, as though some element in the equation were out of place, as though he were at odds with his setting. He almost had to pretend it wasn't there, and he sometimes wished Rahim had filmed him secretly rather than ask for his consent. But why not present for the camera what he willingly disclosed to Rahim? What was it in the camera that troubled him? He thought of Michael Haneke's film *Caché*, in which even innocuous images become horrors, and it occurred to him that perhaps what he most objected to was being watched in absentia, being seen without the possibility of returning the gaze. And what such a vision stood for: that others might see him better, more fully, than he saw himself. Maybe that was a violation, or maybe it was the effect of the real—as in, the camera's ability to simultaneously document and invent reality—that disturbed him.


One night in early February, inspired by the sudden connection to Haneke's film, he twisted the top off a bottle of wine and, although his wife's idea for movie night had been premised on lighter fare, began watching the opening shot of a handsome house on a quiet Parisian street. Well? a man says. Nothing, a woman's voice replies. The scene then shifts to the living room: the couple, Georges and Anne Laurent, have been watching mysterious footage of their own house, and as the story progresses they receive a series of such videos wrapped in plastic bags and accompanied by violent, childish drawings. The footage is innocent enough—it mostly records, without comment, the family's comings and goings. A car moving through the French countryside, then stopping along the road. Or later, the route to a somewhat slummy apartment off Avenue Lénine in the northeastern suburb of Romainville. The apartment is home to a man named Majid, the son of Algerian farm workers, whom Georges's family had planned to adopt some forty years earlier, after the disappearance of his parents.

Until, that is, Georges convinced his own parents to send Majid to an orphanage instead. Majid, when confronted, denies knowing anything about the videos. But shortly thereafter another tape arrives. It's a recording of the conversation they've just had, apparently filmed by a hidden camera in Majid's apartment. In the video, when Georges closes the door behind him, Majid weeps. Some days later, he invites Georges back to his apartment to talk again about the tapes. I wanted you to be present, says Majid, closing the kitchen door, removing a knife from his pocket, and slitting his own throat. Blood splatters on the wall. Georges is dumbstruck. The camera is at the same static angle as in the earlier video. Majid's body blocks the door.

By that point in the film, he had begun to think watching it hadn't been the best idea, maybe even a comically bad one, but his wife had already fallen asleep on the couch beside him—so much for strengthening the bond. The bottle of wine was far from finished, so he poured himself another glass and, against his better judgment, pressed through what passed for a denouement. Majid has a son, but he also denies any part in the videos. While it's almost certainly a lie, by that point it doesn't really matter who's responsible. Then what do you want, Georges asks when the young man confronts him. To know what it's like to have someone's life on your conscience, he replies. Georges is shaken. He goes home in the middle of the day, takes two sleeping pills and closes the shades. In the final scene, with the camera again at a fixed angle, Majid's son visits Georges's, Pierrot, outside his school. He speaks intently, but as viewers we can't hear what he's saying. Do the two know each other? Are they friends? They do seem friendly. Or is this a new phase in the confrontation? Will the sins of the father be visited upon the son? Has Pierrot, who throughout the film is sullen and angry with his parents, been involved in the videos? Or are viewers, in this final scene, back in Georges and Anne's living room, watching yet another terrifying video?

By the end of the third week of classes, he had written himself two more emails documenting the student's erratic behavior. In the reading journal he required his classes to keep, the student's responses aggressively interrogated the validity of specific prompts and proposed that there might even be an ideological agenda at work in asking the class to analyze the course reading. In his first formal essay, the student took his criticism up a notch, concluding in deeply flawed prose that liberal professors were trying to brainwash America's young patriots. The assignment had been to write a personal narrative about a transformative event in one's life, and while the student had started down that path, describing in a vague, cloying manner his performance in the seventh-grade spelling bee, he had given up on the task two-thirds of the way through and its heinous conclusion was not unlike a third arm growing out of one's chest.

When, rather generously, he gave the essay a C, there was a sharp change of tone in the student's journals. He was no longer satisfied with criticizing the prompts and began to criticize their composer. In the fourth and fifth weeks of classes, the student submitted responses in which he questioned the teaching methods, credentials, even the intelligence of his professor. Did he have any real criteria for judging student writing, or was the best he could offer that any given paper wasn't good enough? Weren't they just handing out PhDs these days? Or maybe he had bought it online? He went so far as to suggest that he had been given his degrees solely on the basis of his good looks, which must have fulfilled a quota. Couldn't he see, the student asked, that the class wasn't interested in his long digressions from the material, the stupid little stories from his life with which he punctuated class discussion? They were there to learn how to write, not to hear about how he had been to Paris in 1999, or how, in the 1996 OK-Red conference final, he had received two yellow cards, effectively losing the game for his team.

Even as the student was becoming more animated in writing, in the classroom he was growing increasingly sullen and withdrawn. The hand that had been perpetually raised in the first two weeks was consistently lowered by the sixth. Occasionally, the student would butt into the conversation without being called on, but he was now otherwise silent, which would have been a welcome development if the mounting rage inside him hadn't been palpable. On the one hand, he could sense that the student's psychological state was both building to a fever pitch and above his pay grade, but he also felt he had done nothing to deserve the student's rancor, that the student had been looking for someone or something on which to project the intense discontent that appeared to be consuming his young life. A person who essentially corrected comma errors for a living was as good a target as any.

He first mentioned *Caché* to Rahim in an offhand way, suggesting its dilemma was not entirely separate from his own, but when Rahim asked him to say how, he found he didn't know exactly what he meant, that perhaps he was saying something that only sounded profound but was basically inane. Rahim hadn't seen the film, and given the fuzziness of his own response to it, they quickly let the topic drop, but later that winter Rahim brought it up again. They had been discussing the democratic uprisings known as the Arab Spring. The sight of mass demonstrations, of people struggling toward liberation, stirred something in him. He was inspired, he said, and yet he wondered what lay on the other side of it all, whether the protestors would bring about a new order or whether the forces of repression, having been routed from one place, would gather elsewhere, ready to reassert themselves when the demands of daily life had overtaken everyone once more. It reminds me, Rahim said, of *Caché*—which he had apparently watched, probably with Bill (though not likely with Tony), in the interim—how repression can lodge itself in the psyche, how a trauma can persist over generations.

He had since read on the internet, he told Rahim, how in the early '60s the Paris police, under the direction of Maurice Papon, brutally suppressed a peaceful demonstration for Algerian independence. Hundreds were killed, many beaten to death or thrown off bridges into the Seine. In *Caché*, he said, Majid's parents are supposed to be among the victims, and much as he read Majid's troubled relationship with Georges as an allegory for Algeria's relationship with France, he saw both as a commentary on the antagonism between the West and the Muslim world. When Georges and Anne suspect Majid of having kidnapped their son, for example, TV news plays behind them: helicopters flying above the desert, a street scene of a bombing, possibly in Iraq. And though the TV remains in the background, Haneke situates it in the center of the frame. Rahim wanted to know if he didn't feel a little like Georges, torn between his empathy with the Cairo protestors and the comparably privileged, insular life he led—and if so how to bring the two together, how to tap into the sense of empowerment he felt, channel it in some productive way? They both knew he was cerebral to a fault, but had he ever tried not only to allow himself to feel but to harness the force of a feeling?

He thought about that for a moment. Rahim was pointing to the difference between what he knew about the protests and what he felt as a viewer, which was also the difference between living the news and experiencing it secondhand. Whatever liberation meant for him was not the same as what it meant in Cairo, that much was obvious, but Rahim also seemed to be suggesting that this didn't have to be the case, not completely, that he might catch a feeling as he might catch a wave. But ride it where? Not to Egypt, certainly—that wasn't the point. Daily life, conversely, made for a mundane destination. He couldn't see the use of following a feeling if it only led him back to the conditions that produced it.

His mind quickly went to another place, as it often did, almost as though this were its defense against the difficult task of facing itself, a way to avoid thorny implications. He was thinking of Camus's book, *The Stranger*, he said, but this time Rahim interjected. You're doing it again, Rahim said gently, smiling, by now used to this tic of his, maybe even a little charmed by it. (For a moment he wondered if Rahim found him attractive, wondered if he ever fantasized about fucking his patients, wondered if that was what he was thinking of now, behind that friendly grin.) Weeks earlier, Rahim had put it this way: when it came to the elaborate network of references to which he often resorted, rather than answering Rahim's questions, it was as though he were speaking in half-sentences, leaving off at the conjunction, as though each sentence ended in *and* or *but*. On the other side of that, Rahim believed, were the connections he hadn't yet learned to make, or wasn't willing to. You allow your literary fathers to stand in for you, much as you allow your actual fathers to overshadow your own experience, Rahim had said at the time. Let's push through this, he now added, and get to the other side.

When the magistrate asks, he began, whether Meursault, in custody for murdering an unnamed Arab, felt sad on the day of his mother's unrelated death, he responds that he had pretty much lost the habit of analyzing himself and so it was hard for him to tell the man what he wanted to know. During his subsequent trial, he spots a bright-eyed reporter watching him and has the odd impression of being observed by himself. Then, in the closing argument, his lawyer speaks about him in the first person: It is true I killed a man, the lawyer says, but to Meursault the lawyer's speech is a way to exclude him even further from the case, reducing him to nothing, and, in a sense, substituting himself for Meursault. If something is going to happen to me, I want to be there, he says, as though he were a witness to and not a participant in his own life—and this while considering that his head would soon, and in the name of the French people, be chopped off. It's this psychological death that ultimately concerns Camus, he said, more so than the physical one—the condition that appears to shirk self-examination but in fact precludes it. In other words, *The Stranger*, like *Caché*, may have less to do with the distance between Algeria and France than with the distance between Meursault and himself.

And now you need to admit it, Rahim said, with a force that surprised him. This is how you feel, like you're witnessing your life from a distance, that there's a chasm running through the center of it that you haven't found a way to cross. Yes, he said softly, a little chastened. That's it exactly.


By the seventh week of class, the student had stopped submitting his journals through the online portal. At the beginning of the eighth, he did, however, submit his second essay, a bizarre profile of a Christian debating club in which the student described the members as a new breed of Americans who, paradoxically, would rebuild the nation with the Truth on which it was founded. They were holy terrors, as dangerous as they were scrupulous, the student wrote in his conclusion, which he imagined being written in a fit of inspiration, as the student was stirred to new heights of madness by whatever nationalistic claptrap he had heard that day on talk radio. The essay was worse than bad, though he recognized that there was perhaps an unintentional, satirical brilliance in its stupidity. Considering that it was half the length he had stipulated and that it barely addressed the prompt, he had seen no other option but to fail the student on the assignment.

This unleashed a veritable shit storm, as he might have imagined it would. The next thing he knew he was being summoned to a meeting by the department chair to discuss the situation, which had exploded into the dean's office when the student's father had heaped an unprecedented invective on the campus administration. Both the dean and the chair were in the latter's corner office, with its double bank of windows facing the mountains to the west and south, when he arrived for their meeting. The father, they told him, had been livid, and if he thought the student was a piece of work, the young man was a mere shadow of his apeshit father, who had gone so far as to suggest that he might be the sort of teacher who shows up to class one day and opens fire on his students. It had been a strange, twisted distortion of what was plain to everyone in the room: the student posed a real threat. But the father, in the haze, the chair suspected, of Tea Party rhetoric, had sought to project this threat away from his son, onto the teacher, in a perversion of an all-too-common phenomenon that was as deeply offensive to him, he could see, as it was to the authorities in the room.

It was at this point he disclosed that he had been keeping a time-stamped log of the student's behavior, and that he had also saved each of the student's journal postings and papers. The chair exchanged a glance with the dean, who had mostly been silent. They shared a look of surprise and, he thought, relief. They would need him to turn that material over to them at once, the chair said. They would take it from here. And the student, he asked, what would happen to him? They'd been bitten before, the dean said, finally speaking up. He was a balding Latino man in his early fifties with the somewhat unpleasant habit of tugging at his closely trimmed goatee. They made an odd pair, the dour dean and acid chair, whose long, prematurely gray hair made her look a bit like an aging Joni Mitchell. There had been an incident several years ago, the dean said, when a local Fox affiliate had picked up a story about an adjunct professor who had encouraged his students to analyze the public persona of Sarah Palin, then running for vice president. There had been a showdown between a disgruntled student and the administration, and the overblown Fox segment was picked up by the newspapers. They were surprised he hadn't heard about it. The dean said that, given the familiarity of the student's profile, the school was worried about a repeat. But, no, the chair said, you shouldn't expect to see him again, and if you do please inform us immediately. She then asked whether he knew the number for campus security, which the dean proceeded to write on the back of his business card, along with his cellphone number. We'll know more in the next few days, he said, but if we make it through the weekend, we should be in the clear, although as they stood up to shake hands, drawing the brief meeting to a close, he realized he had almost no idea what the dean meant.

In the following weeks, Rahim had returned to this idea of a chasm, the gaps between actual and imagined experience, and between his emotional and intellectual lives. The gaps were not the same but functioned in parallel ways, cordoning off what he felt from what he knew, what he wrote from how he lived. The distinctions appeared increasingly trifling, even though the dissonances they produced—between him and his family, for instance—were not. They also returned to the metaphor of the trial and to the notion of a defense that was only absurd, they both agreed, because it was ultimately unnecessary. It was as though Rahim was trying to push his buttons, to soften him up, maybe get him to finally tug at the box of tissues. What did he have to prove, Rahim asked, but the verb cut two ways, suggesting both evidence and worth. He admired this carefulness on Rahim's part, this exactitude that was so effective it almost seemed scripted, and he wondered whether it was, whether Rahim, having watched his videos of their sessions, knew what he was going to say before he said it and so could prepare his responses in advance. He was comforted to think that someone whose life, at least on the surface, so little resembled his own might understand him this fully. The real trouble, he thought in that moment, was that the only feelings he'd ever been interested in understanding, albeit at a distance, were his own, and that his inability to understand himself, a product of the chasms he had nurtured, was also precisely the cause of his unwillingness to engage with the feelings of others.

I'm thinking again, Rahim said, of *Caché*: Georges feels he's being watched, but by whom? Well, he said to Rahim, if he's under surveillance, he's also—insomuch as he watches the videos—the one conducting it. But where others would see a fairly straightforward presentation of his life, Georges sees something more sinister, Rahim added. And was this happening for him? Was he seeking and finding proof where there wasn't any? Proof of what, he asked. You tell me, Rahim prodded. As viewers, he responded, we are also watching a recording, and just as Georges is troubled by the mirror held up to his life perhaps we are troubled by the realism of the film, the mirror it holds up to our insular and secure yet deeply complicit lives. But this fictional space is further mirrored, or refracted, by the surveillance films: it's as though *Caché* arrived at our door wrapped in a childish drawing. Are we watching ourselves watch ourselves here? And what to make of it, he mused, if our experiences— *your* experiences, Rahim interrupted—if *my* experiences fail to be real unless I see them displayed on a screen or written on a page?

And so, Rahim asked, steering him, do you see how this connects to your grandfather? He thought about that for a moment before saying that in the cabin he might have been writing about his own suicide, the one he only allowed himself to contemplate through the proxy of his relative. And then, almost on cue, Rahim was finally handing him the tissues.


After the situation with the student had finally been resolved, Rahim had asked whether he saw similarities between his own story and the young man's. Did he mean the heavy-handed father, he asked, the son living in his shadow? That was hardly his experience, he said, as his own father had always been the opposite sort of man, kind and generous to a fault. I'm not talking about your father, Rahim said. There was a long but not unpleasant pause before either of them spoke. Imagine being this student, Rahim said, having his father as your own. And then he added, almost out of nowhere, your grandfather's story isn't yours.

But is it my student's, he asked, or some version of it, anyway? He sensed in the student, and in his father's support of him, a deep distrust of the intellect, of intellectuals, and of questions for which there weren't clear-cut answers, let alone an approach to the world premised on entertaining such questions. If everything were open to scrutiny, then nothing could be taken for granted, and the danger he posed, he realized, was the ability to turn certainties into doubts. It wasn't as though he relished the task, he said, and much of his struggle, such as it was, stemmed from the fact that everything in his own life was constantly being called into question, that everything he thought and felt, or thought he felt or felt he thought, was under an ongoing process of revision.

Then again, the fracas had also been an excuse on the father's part to get a refund for a class his son was failing, a class for which he had become unsuited as a result of the poisoned ideology he had probably been spoon-fed since he was small. He wasn't sure whether the gambit had worked, however, wasn't sure what the final outcome had been. He only knew that, according to an email from the chair, he was now, a month after their meeting, in the clear. She thanked him for what she called his stand-up conduct, said that nothing more would be required of him, but that if he wanted to debrief, if only to get some closure, she would gladly meet again. And did he want closure? Rahim asked. Had they met again? It was a funny story, he said. He had arranged for a second meeting, but as he was driving on the highway his car had broken down, the clutch had given out, though he didn't know that at the time, and he had had to call the chair to cancel the meeting from underneath an overpass. They had yet to reschedule.

As winter quickly turned to spring, he found himself reading Freud's essay on the uncanny, Freud's peculiar kind of fright, rooted in what was once well known and had long been familiar. Following Freud, he traced the etymological paths by which the German word *unheimlich* became equated with its antonym, *heimlich*, and by which home became conflated with foreignness.

On one level Majid, like Meursault, serves as a double: Majid as the substitute son, driven down a divergent path; Meursault as the godless, alienated version of the reader. Like all doubles, both trouble any sense of self. They're proof that a person may identify himself with another and so become unsure of his true self, or substitute the other's self for his own—proof that the self may be duplicated, divided, and interchanged. Initially, Freud writes, such doubling was a defense against annihilation: the body found safe haven in the soul, and heaven became a double for earth. Having once been an assurance of immortality, however, for rationalistic minds the double becomes the harbinger of death. And if, as Freud writes, the uncanny describes everything that was intended to remain secret and has come into the open—if it arises when something we had forgotten was real becomes so again—then generations also become vehicles for the uncanny. In that our borders blur. In that we are not our own. In that my body is bigger than I am, he thought: it belongs to my child, my genes, my parents, their parents, my death. The double is a repetition, and in fathering a son he had doubled a portion of his genes, combining them with his wife's, which is also to say that their son would repeat them both, as they were repeating their parents, and their parents' parents, and so on, through successive generations: the constant recurrence of the same thing, the repetition of the same facial features, the same characters, the same destinies, the same misdeeds, even the same names.

Still, by late March the weather had warmed and with it his mood. Rahim noted the change in him. His condition—Rahim didn't like the word *pathology*—had improved considerably. He was learning to tell kinder, more productive stories about himself, Rahim said. There were fewer unicorns in them, anyway, fewer bugbears. He wondered whether Rahim missed the sun on days like these. Wouldn't it be better if there were a window where the landscape hung on the opposite wall? Didn't he like the painting, Rahim asked, laughing a little. He scrutinized the image, as though seeing it for the first time. It seemed to be early morning in the picture, and a light mist clung to the ground. It wasn't a particularly noteworthy painting, he said after a moment, but then he imagined that was the point. It was a place for the eyes to rest. Like the visual equivalent of elevator music, he said. And yet maybe I could step from the office into the world of the painting, my shoes dampening as I walked across the grass, toward the trees, my son jogging along at my side, and who's to say what we might find there, what monsters might be lurking in the shadows? I take back what I said, Rahim joked. You're clearly doing worse.

He would be gone the following week, he told Rahim, on a trip to see his in-laws in Florida, and the week after that a famous novelist would be in town giving a talk during their normal meeting time. They agreed that he would call the week he returned to set up their next visit, but once outside he knew, as grateful as he was, that he wouldn't call. That, for whatever reason, they were finished for now, despite his certainty that there was still work to be done. Sometimes it was better to go out on a high note, he thought, to leave some problems unsolved, some avenues unexplored.

Robins were hopping about in the small strip of grass between the row of empty elliptical trainers and the street, and he wondered whether one would again build a nest in the tree outside his kitchen window. It isn't so much that time heals all wounds, he thought, walking to his recently repaired Subaru, as it is that time guides a wound from its primary into its secondary and tertiary effects. Later: malaise. Later: anxiety. Later: fanaticism or a fanatical desire to drown in the bottom of a glass. This is not exactly what he thought. There were mirrors in his mind: they showed him as Georges, as Meursault, as Majid.

## 3

It was soon summer and I was again trying to order my notes into some semblance of legibility. Spring had been a long, unproductive season, and I was avoiding a more direct confrontation with the heap of words that had not, as yet, coalesced, removing a sentence here, changing a verb tense there. I took heart from Georges Perec, who writes that his books follow a path, mark out a space, trace a tentative itinerary, describe point by point the stages of a search the why of which he can't tell, only the how. I believe, he says, that I discover—I prove—the direction I am moving in by moving. It's an optimistic act, not to know where you're heading and to head there anyway; doing so helps you be fully who (and where) you are. Perhaps I had up until then lacked the necessary optimism, or perhaps the whole time I had been going precisely nowhere.

Early one morning I woke from a dream in which my father gave me his copy of the *Chuang Tzu*, the eponymous text by the Chinese philosopher from the fourth century BCE. I had read it years ago in college, but since then a few remarkable passages had rattled around in my memory. In one, Chuang Tzu dreams he is a butterfly only to wake up reminded that he is a man. So real was the dream of flitting from flower to flower, however, that he cannot determine with any certainty whether he was a man dreaming of being a butterfly or whether he is now a butterfly dreaming of being a man. My own dream was no doubt a distortion of the time my father gave me, when I was still a teenager, a copy of Lao Tzu's famous *Tao Te Ching*, except in the dream my father's *Chuang Tzu* was marked up with marginal notes in my own handwriting. Is this text dreaming me? I wondered. It is only through writing that I become myself, Werner Herzog says, but this bringing into being is also a bringing into banality, and the I that appears on the page may only be real to the extent that it has become a commonplace. Not a butterfly, but a man sitting in a dark basement, quite early in the morning, as the day gathers above him. At the same time, how *strange* this man appeared to me now, so little did he resemble the butterflies of my dreams. I almost wanted to call him an abstraction, this figure bent over the computer, but that would be even *stranger*: an abstract actualization. Such is the position of the subject: foreign at the moment it becomes concrete.

In fact my father had sent me, not long before, a book that arrived one Monday morning in early February. It was an unexpected present, and I read it off and on during a flight to Cincinnati, then on my connection to DC. Somewhere over Pennsylvania, I read a classroom exchange in which the teacher follows up on his assertion that an essay requires digressions, depends on them for total effect. They're discussing the scene from *The Catcher in the Rye* in which Holden's class is instructed to shout Digression! whenever a speaker strays from his topic. What's Salinger saying? the teacher asks. That digressions are the best parts, one student offers. But if you only digress, another responds, you'll lose the thread, fly off into space. It's like the blues, a third student adds. You can depart from the melody for only so long before you lose the tune and, with it, the listener.

I read the book dutifully, delighted that Dad thought to buy it for me, even if I disagreed with some of its advice. When I failed to finish it on the plane, I toted it around with me that evening as I rode the Metro to meet an old friend at a restaurant near DuPont Circle—one of his favorites, he said over the phone. Perhaps it was my inborn resistance to guidance, but as I stepped onto the endless escalator at the station I found myself wanting to write an essay that digressed even from its digressions, that lost its thread over and over because its point was not a thread but a life.


I was in DC for a conference, but I was equally there to see Oliver, a friend I had made in my early twenties when we were both waiting tables for a living and avoiding the messy business of what to do with our lives. I had liked Oliver immediately. Odd non sequiturs sprang from his lips, as though he were always two or three steps ahead of the conversation. What Oliver knew he had learned from observing plants, animals, and the systems through which they interacted. I admired this rootedness in him, and when I left Ann Arbor for graduate school I missed it. Oliver followed suit not long after and began a peculiar program of research, which, as he explained that evening, had raised the hackles of many in his department. At issue was not his science itself, but what had pejoratively been called his philosophizing. His mentor had been supportive, but elsewhere he had encountered fierce resistance to his project, which was invested in bringing science out of the academic journals. You see, he said, our problem is not so different from yours. Specialization is a kind of cocoon, and when the other larvae see you breaking out they get defensive.

Our number was called and, after picking up our food at the front counter, we sat at a table in the cramped second-floor dining room. The building struck me as an odd place for a restaurant; from the outside, it looked as if it had once housed an embassy. Inside, however, the colors were warm, and the walls displayed the work of a local photographer— cityscapes, mostly, with the occasional portrait. As we ate our bowls of udon, Oliver asked about my work, and I told him, in a shorthand way, about Herzog, about the cabin, and about my notion of estrangement. Oliver wondered whether I remembered the biologist Sam Bowser from another Herzog film, *Encounters at the End of the World*. Bowser's team is engaged in deep-sea dives beneath the ice sheet, he explained, where they are observing species that live sealed off from the world above. In the film, Bowser describes several varieties of foraminifera or forams—small protists that live along the seabed. They have a system of pseudopodia they use to eat and to move—long, tubular strands that extend from the cell wall—but are most remarkable for the tiny shells they produce, called *tests*. As they gather material from their surroundings to build them, they select certain particles and reject other, less suitable ones. It's almost art, Bowser says. Herzog then asks—with great care, Herzog says— whether Bowser would call them intelligent. Bowser cites in response the case of the mystic, microscopist, and scholar Edward Heron-Allen.

Heron-Allen wasn't trained as a scientist, Oliver explained, but as a lawyer, and in addition to his study of foraminifera, he also translated works from Persian, wrote books on palmistry and local history, and produced, under the pseudonym Christopher Blayre, a series of stories somewhere between science fiction and horror. More remarkable yet, Oliver told me that in 1885 Heron-Allen published a celebrated book, continuously in print since its first edition, the full title of which—as I later looked up—is *Violin-Making: As It Was and Is: Being a Historical, Theoretical, and Practical Treatise on the Science and Art of Violin-Making for the Use of Violin Makers and Players, Amateur and Professional.*

It's funny you mention Herzog, Oliver said, because this other film has everything to do with my work. In 1915, he continued, when Heron-Allen, as the newly elected president of the Royal Microscopical Society, suggested that forams possessed faculties akin to intelligence, the members of that august body were appalled. Under pressure from his peers, Heron-Allen later backed away from his claim, which had proposed two criteria for intelligence. First: the forams selected certain materials and rejected others for the construction of their tests. Second: they applied these materials in highly sophisticated ways. But at some point, Oliver told me, experiments comparable to the mouse in the maze were conducted. The protists couldn't remember where the cheese was. The real trouble with saying forams are intelligent, however, as Heron-Allen discovered, is that it introduces certain anthropomorphic suggestions that arise out of the word *intelligence* itself. The word carries too much human baggage; we can't apply it to animals without thinking of ourselves.

The larger question, he said, is how we divide human from non-human life and what this division entails. Certain members of my department tell me it's a better topic for a psychologist or a philosopher, but for my part I want to see the forams within a continuum that ranges from the smallest expressions of life to the largest. And more importantly: if human activity, everything from books to buildings, is basically no different than the agglutinating matter in the forams' shells—that is to say, a product of selection and application—at what point does experience cease to produce a test? Order subordinates, he said. Definitions divide. To say one species is not another may be a straightforward distinction, but to say how—or, more problematically, why—the human species has *risen above* the rest of creation is trickier territory.

By then we had finished our meals and were leaning back in our chairs. Oliver had an early meeting in the morning but said he had time for a beer or two if we wanted to walk down the block. We took the side streets in the general direction of the station from which, in a couple of hours, I would ride the Metro back to my hotel by the airport. We crossed over Connecticut Avenue and walked down a few steps into a cavernous underground bar lined entirely in wood. Oliver brought a round over to a small table along the back wall, and though we had spoken of lighter things as we walked—mutual friends, the drizzle— once situated in the bar we returned to our earlier conversation.

The Italian philosopher Giorgio Agamben, Oliver said, believes that the boundaries between man and animal are more arbitrary than they appear. He doesn't go so far as to suggest some mystical connection between all forms of life, but he's concerned about how, on one hand, these boundaries reflect political realities and, on the other, how they reverberate in the psychological makeup of human beings. We must learn, Agamben writes, said Oliver, to think of man as what results from the incongruity of these two elements (the human and the animal), and investigate not the metaphysical mystery of conjunction, but rather the practical and political mystery of separation. For what is man if he is always the place—and, at the same time, the result—of ceaseless divisions and caesurae?

It is more urgent to work on these divisions, Agamben believes, to ask in what way the animal has been separated from the human, than it is to take positions on the great issues, on so-called human rights and values. It's not that these things are unimportant, Oliver said, but before we can address our shitty pay, shabby health care, lousy schools, and the ongoing ecological holocaust—before we can fix a Haiti or Kinshasa—we have to understand that our meatpackers have become extensions of the cattle that cycle through feedlots, slaughterhouses, and supermarkets. We have to recognize how people in Haiti and the Congo, among others, founder in structures that define but don't ameliorate their conditions. And then there are the animals we have come to think of, on the other side of their cage walls or secreted away in their preserves, as subordinate to the human world. It's hubris to think a species may be saved or the warming of the planet stopped, but it may also miss the point. There is no mastery. We are not creation's saviors. And so, Oliver chuckled, all that remains is the complete rethinking of the categories of life.

I went to order another round, and when I returned Oliver was still smiling. So, he asked, clinking his glass with mine, are you going to put this in your book? I told him I wasn't sure what animal intelligence had to do with it. Had I ever said my son was acting like an animal? When his own son, Lucas, was born he couldn't get over it. I kept telling Molly, he said, that this was animal life, this was the closest to an animal he would ever get. She wasn't convinced, but then we started reading to him. In children's books, Oliver claimed, animals act in revealing ways. Take *Carl's Birthday*, for instance: Carl the Rottweiler and Madeleine the toddler unwrap presents and add sugar to the punchbowl. They even manage to fill up a helium balloon in the shape of a reindeer. It's as if the two were living on the same existential plane, a humiliating proposition for either one, perhaps, depending on how you look at it. And then there's *Are You My Mother?* Do you know it? A mother bird feels her egg beginning to jump. After she leaves to find food, the bird hatches. It asks a kitten, a hen, a cow, and a dog whether each is its mother. Before long, it comes across an excavator; naturally, the baby bird asks the machine if it's its mother. No driver is visible, but the contraption picks up the bird and drops it back in the nest just in time for its mother to arrive with a tasty worm. I'm still figuring out, Oliver said, what to make of the fact that while everything else is rendered in dull colors, shades of brown mostly, the backhoe is bright red—and that, unlike the talking animals, the machine can only snort. But industry will save you.

I said it might be because of interpretations like his that many children's books—books like *Goodnight Moon* and *Brown Bear, Brown Bear, What Do You See?*—eschew plot altogether. They favor formulaic structures instead, in which each page is a different version of the preceding one: even though you can't get some of these books out of your head, once you figure out the formula, you can relax. Nothing's going to happen that hasn't already. A brown bear sees a red bird, a red bird sees a yellow duck, who might then ask a turtle, a frog, or a fish whether they've seen a stray moose. As much as I was tempted to read this as a lesson about narrative, Oliver was more interested in the way these books make the natural world conform to the human one. Of course the animals speak, he said. Of course they have consciousness. Because if we didn't recognize ourselves in them—and in the natural world of which they are a part—we would be outcasts or bastards in their midst, instead of vice versa. Whether or not the authors intend to, he went on, they encourage a cuddly version of the animal world, one that teaches children to be friends with nature even as they're conditioned (sometimes subtly, sometimes not) to become its masters. People talk about raising their children, but they mean something like raising them above their animal impulses, their urges and emotions. The sooner a child sees an animal as human, the sooner he recognizes that an animal is not human—that the human is above the animal, the rational above the irrational. So we're back to that, I said. We're back to that, Oliver said.

But the fact is, he continued, it takes very little to turn us into animals again. Did I ever tell you, he asked, suddenly serious, about our intruder? He hadn't, I said, and even in the dim light of the bar Oliver's face turned pale for a moment. He began to tell me how, the previous summer, there had been a break-in at their apartment. He and Molly had been asleep when she awoke to a noise coming from the kitchen. She shook him and whispered that someone was in the house. Oliver told her she was imagining things and turned over in bed, but she was insistent. You're the man, go see what's happening, she said. Oliver thought about that for a moment before standing and walking out into the hall. In a sleepy haze, he could vaguely make out a figure moving toward him and telling him firmly but quietly to sit the fuck down. He had a gun, Oliver said, or at least what, in the dark hallway, looked like one. The man peered into the bedroom and waved Molly out of it. He pushed her down next to Oliver. The two of them, he said, were shaking. Don't hurt us, Molly kept repeating. Don't hurt our son.

She was sobbing softly, and the man, who had not likely counted on them waking up but was nonetheless prepared for it, led them into the living room. As he quickly duct-taped their hands, ankles, and mouths, whatever made them human receded into the distance. We were back in the primordial soup our ancestors had evolved lungs and legs to crawl out of, Oliver said, where it was all fight or flight, kill or be killed.

The intruder worked efficiently, avoiding Lucas's room altogether. On the kitchen table, he stacked their laptops and phones and some of Molly's jewelry—he had found the diamond earrings her mother had given her but which she was too ashamed to wear. In the dim light trickling from the other rooms, they could make out his silhouette but not his face. Before long, he turned off the lights in the bedroom and office and went into the kitchen, where they saw the refrigerator open and shut several times. They heard plates rattling, then he emerged carrying a sandwich and a small backpack, presumably with their things in it. The backpack he placed by the door, but he carried the sandwich over to the living room. He sat on a chair opposite the couch where, to the extent it was possible, Molly and Oliver had regained their composure.

It was a bad time to be leaving the neighborhood with a lot of stolen property, the man explained. His voice was well modulated, an educated voice. He would wait until five, he said, when there would be more people about. Oliver looked at the clock. It was four. I have no interest in hurting you, the man said. This—he lifted up the revolver as though it were the heaviest object in the world and returned it to his lap—is just a tool, no different from a hammer at the end of the day. He complimented them, Oliver said, on the arrangement of their apartment. Very Zen, he called it. The three of them sat in silence as he ate his sandwich. Sweat was loosening the duct tape on Oliver's mouth, but he couldn't imagine calling for help.

Eventually, the man heaved a large sigh. He said he could see they were good people. He felt he owed them an explanation. This was the shape of it: there was nothing for him to do. He had resisted at first but only recently had realized how foolish his resistance had been. If I'm smart, he told them, I can do this for a few years and disappear—

Brazil, maybe, or Thailand. And if I get caught, well, I have no illusions about any of this. My condition is my defense, not that the courts will care. He spoke in a general way about his upbringing, which sounded, Oliver told me, rather middle class. The intruder claimed to have done well in school, and even to have graduated college with a degree in theater. Oliver didn't know what, if any of it, to believe, but the man was convincing enough. He never apologized, Oliver said, but there was something apologetic in his tone. Soon, it was nearly five and the man carried his dirty dish into the kitchen; they could hear him placing it in the sink. When he left not long after, Oliver hopped off to get the scissors. They took turns cutting each other loose.

There were ongoing investigations, the policemen said later that morning, and yes, there had been other robberies. The whole experience rattled Molly, and in the weeks that followed she started to see a therapist. After a few months, she came home one day from a session and told Oliver that if the intruder were ever caught they couldn't press charges. That really shocked me, he said. Here she had been so terrified and angry, and then to come home having transformed that into something generous. She had realized, she told him, that there was no way to make the intruder leave her mind now that he had entered it. He was there, and she had to make a home for him. Things were replaceable, but the man's life was not. Oliver had gone out and bought a new computer the day of the robbery, and he had thought at the time how strange it was that what had been so difficult for the intruder to acquire had, after a phone call to his insurance agent, been immediately resupplied to him. That capitalism keeps even its semi-successful agents happy—Molly was a lawyer, after all—came as no surprise to Oliver. More startling was the way the theft had been treated by everyone involved—the police, the neighbors, the insurance agent—as an animal act.

Even more troubling was the question Oliver had refused to answer to nearly everybody who asked, excepting the police: that of the man's race. There had been something insinuated that he couldn't quite stomach. The animal experience, in any case, had been Molly and Oliver's, not the intruder's. He had been perfectly rational, genial even, whereas Molly and Oliver, according to him, had been overcome by impulses and emotions they had rarely experienced and didn't understand. Oliver had been so taken by the poignancy of it that he had, for a moment, misunderstood the neighbor who in hearing the story had whispered, *animals*. He had thought the neighbor was talking about him.

We were both a little drunk by then, Oliver and I, but it was getting late. As we stood to go, I speculated about how the case of the intruder compared to that of the stranger. I would think, Oliver said, they are almost identical.


Several months came and went. By the time I got around to dreaming about the *Chuang Tzu*, it was an unbearably hot summer in Colorado, the warmest on record. Almost no rain fell, and the tomato plants my wife and I were growing had been struck by some kind of blight I kept calling heatstroke, over her considerable protests. We used poor soil, I said portentously, as though I were talking about something more serious. We had only ourselves to blame. Quit being so dramatic, she said.

But in Michigan, too, the weather was so balmy that my mother's father, who had stubbornly refused to turn on his air conditioning, needed to be hospitalized. After a frightening couple of days during which a number of diagnoses were bandied about, ranging from a bowel obstruction to colon cancer, it was decided he had simply overheated. The attending physician told him it was no longer safe for him to live on his own, that his age had gotten the better of his judgment, and that it was now a question of his safety. Later that summer I read, as I knew I would each year after, that Arctic ice levels were at their lowest point in recorded history, and I could not help but draw a connection, which this time my wife did not immediately reject, between the words of my grandfather's doctor and those of the scientists who said that humanity was no longer capable of acting in its best interest, if it ever had been.

As I continued to wrangle my notes on strangeness, I often found myself thinking about Oliver, and I wondered, on the daily walks I took with my son, whether the text accumulating on my desk was not the line that separated the two of us, or that separated us both from the animals—whether my writing itself was to blame for my ongoing crisis. We are not wasps or robins, I thought. Culture encodes, or inscribes, our lessons, and whereas evolution has always required that a species internalize its history, human intelligence may consist in an ability to externalize it. That summer, I started to see genomes as scriptoriums, and I considered that, as our distinguishing characteristic, language may have grown as much out of a need to bypass evolution's time-consuming mechanisms as it did out of a fear of saber-tooth tigers. If it's the case that, in language, evolution evolved beyond itself, then language may also be an evolutionary paradox—a trait that allows those who possess it to sidestep the thing that made it possible—and the irremediable gap between human and animal life, which Oliver so thoroughly interrogates, comes into a different focus: while other species continue to evolve through normal channels, we've discovered a shortcut. It may also be that, biologically, we have ceased to evolve, or more optimistically, that there is no precedent for the type of evolution we are undergoing. It's one of a few things for which we still lack the right words.

When I wrote this and more in an email to Oliver, he mostly ignored the point I was trying to get at about our emotions; how they share the same pathways as thought and so may be another form of thinking, albeit one almost impossible to render in intellectual terms, which is to say *in words*. Given the gravity of my recent depression, I could see that what followed, what I had in fact initiated, was possibly a ridiculous exchange, how inept the two of us were, at least with each other, at speaking of anything that mattered, even as we spoke only of what mattered. Why even bother having a life, I asked myself, if I hid from it in my thinking?

Oliver responded, as though we were still sitting at the bar, that he, like Agamben, wasn't interested in producing a better definition of either human or animal; his goal was to understand how these definitions work and to render inoperative the systems that produce them. But if distinguishing man from non-man has been an endless source of trouble, Oliver wrote, the alternative is to live between such distinctions, which is to say *outside* them. Smart people have told me that cities are not *natural*; *wilderness*, they say, exists in the mountains, the deserts, even the oceans. But nature isn't relegated to the national parks; the animal is not the being that lives on the other side of the glass. One might refuse to see our houses as the tests they are, but what to say about the six thousand birds from fifty-five species counted by volunteers one recent Sunday in Central Park? Neither nature nor civilization, so-called, begins or ends at the ranger station; the station articulates both. It's hard to say what the world would look like if we situated ourselves in this profound neither/nor, Oliver wrote, but perhaps rather than simply risking ourselves in that divide we would find ourselves responsible to both sides of it, with a foot facing toward each world but belonging to neither. Then he added that this had obvious implications for strangeness: who are you, he asked, if not both the arbiter and embodiment of your lineage? Who are you if not a creature with one foot in your head and one in your heart?

That night in the bar, Oliver's point had been that life is not a procession of fixed categories. It is not the rigid hierarchy that has defined taxonomy since its beginnings. But as we walked back to the Metro, his descriptions of his research, now that he had several drinks in him, sounded less like the work of a serious scientist and more like the musings of a slightly cracked mystic. When I said as much Oliver laughed. To him, the best science walked a thin line between metaphor and fact, and he had long ago left behind any affinity for researchers who didn't ask questions larger than the scope of their studies. I should read Lynn Margulis, he said, who believes life is a question the universe poses to itself in the form of a human being. She argues that our intelligence is embedded in life as a whole, which consists of a single, expanding network, and in which humans behave as the brain or neural tissue. But life is also teleological, she says. It strives. And it will continue without us. The bacteria from which it first evolved may very well have to start all over again, but no amount of carbon dioxide is going to obliterate them. The science is solid, he said, but she's always asking herself, what's the significance? We scientists often can't see further than the microscopes in front of us. Or mass spectrometers, I suggested. Oliver laughed again, but by then we were back at the huge escalator that descended into the depths below Connecticut Avenue. We wished each other luck and parted ways, and it was only when I was comfortably in my seat on the train that I realized I was still carrying, as an amulet maybe, the book my father had given me, *Unless It Moves the Human Heart*, and that, earlier in the evening, I had meant to ask Oliver what biological basis there might be for an essay that flies off into space.

## 4

From his hotel in Crystal City, he took the yellow line to Archives Station, where, after the long escalator ride up to street level, he was so discombobulated by the unfamiliar buildings that he walked for fifteen minutes in the wrong direction before stopping a well-dressed man on the street and asking him the way. Soon enough he found himself on another of the broad avenues plaguing the city, in front of the National Gallery of Art. He had not come to the museum, as was often the case, with any painting or exhibition in mind, and as a result he spent an inordinate amount of time walking slowly through early American landscapes before sitting down in front of a painting he had never seen before, by an artist he knew only by name. It depicted a young woman in consummate luxury, reclining on a sofa under a large, wall-sized painting. At first, he didn't pay much attention to the woman across from him on the bench, but after a few moments he found himself drawn to the large and small movements of her arms as she translated the image into her sketchbook. He had only sat there out of exhaustion, but watching the image take on a new life through her he came to love Sargent's painting—an experience that, watching other sketchers working in other galleries, he has not been able to duplicate since.

When, without looking up from her work, she asked whether he liked Sargent, he realized she must have been aware of his attention the entire time. Only then, as he clumsily told her (in what must have sounded like a pick-up line) that he liked him now, did he finally comprehend the long scarf tied around her head and trailing, in place of her hair, down to the middle of her back. It's a painting of his niece, Rose-Marie, she told him. This one was done before the war, she said, when she would have been about twenty. That makes sense, he said. She turned to look at him over the rims of her glasses, as though she couldn't believe he was continuing the charade. Such a painting would have been inconceivable after the war, he offered. She sighed and relaxed a little then, as though he had passed a test. What else do you see in it, she asked, almost facetiously. A critique, he said, of the laziness and self-satisfaction of the age. Her nonchalance is the pose of the time—a mixture of poetry, privilege, and boredom. Her husband died in the war, she replied, just a few years after the painting was finished. A few years after that, she was attending Good Friday services in Paris when a German shell struck the church, killing her and seventy others. She paused, moved, he supposed, by the sadness of it, then said that around the time he was painting it—she gestured to the canvas in front of them—Sargent called portraiture a pimp's profession. He had sworn off any new commissions, and so this, presumably, was his answer to a challenge he had set for himself: to paint portraits that were not overtly experimental in the manner of Matisse or Picasso but which—like the paintings of Bonnard in a way, she said—used more traditional approaches to seeing the world anew.

She stopped drawing and looked down at what she had done. Can you tell I do this for a living, she said. You're a tour guide, he asked, glancing at her lively sketch once more. Something like that, she said dryly—I help direct the education programs. Must be interesting work, he said. It has its benefits, she said. They spoke for maybe fifteen minutes—about his own work, the conference, parenthood—when she asked suddenly if he had eaten lunch. He hadn't, he said, and after introducing herself as Naomi, she invited him to join her in the underground café between the old wing, where they were sitting, and the new one. Something about standing, how it elongates the body, made him realize how drawn and gaunt her features were, but also that not even the ravages of her disease had annulled the beauty of her face.

Downstairs, the café was surprisingly bright and airy, the food surprisingly appealing. He told her that, like much else he had seen in DC, the tunnel between the two wings struck him as a scene from some futuristic dystopia à la Philip K. Dick. She laughed. There's more to DC than this hallway, she said, and a lot of it you wouldn't want to see. It's ironic, she continued, that the nation's capital also has its worst schools. I send my daughters to a private one and it kills me. They collected their food from the cafeteria-style stations and found a table next to a long line of large planters. They tell you, she said, forcing a spoonful of soup into her mouth, to eat several smaller meals, but it doesn't really help. I can't imagine, he said. You don't want to, she replied. And the prognosis? he asked. She shook her head and told him that the worst part, the unbearable part, was the thought that her young daughters, five and seven, might grow up without a mother. But it was even worse than that, she said. When I imagine them graduating high school or going out on dates, when I imagine them in college or in crisis, or beginning to raise their own children, the thought that I might be absent from any of it makes me feel as though my chest will explode. You must be very strong, he said, not knowing what else to say. It's funny, she said, but it's the thought of them without me that gives me strength.

When they had finished eating, he sat there drinking his coffee as she talked—none for me, she had said. Her voice was soft but self-assured. Kevin, her husband, had been supportive, the best, in fact, but she could see how diminished she was in his eyes and that nearly destroyed her. You know, she said, when you sat next to me I remembered a feeling I used to have. Now, when heads turn, it's to see whether this—she pulled the fabric over one shoulder—is really a scarf. He thought for a moment of telling her that she was still an attractive woman, maybe even that he found her attractive, but he didn't know how it would sound coming out of a stranger's mouth, a married one at that. He briefly imagined the two of them fucking in a nearby bathroom, Naomi's skirt around her waist, her back against the wall, but he had never been the forward sort, knew how ludicrous, for many reasons, this vision was. Terrible manners, he thought, forcing himself to tune back in. I even come here on my days off, she was saying. It's strange, but before the diagnosis I spent almost no time in the galleries anymore. I was so busy with work and the kids. I had almost forgotten what it was like to walk through the place, to lose yourself in it. That was what drew me to art in the first place, the idea that I could be—what's the word?—*subsumed* by an image. She had been a painter, she told him, a decent one, but had known she could never make a living doing it. So in college she switched her major to art education, then she went on to get a graduate degree in museum studies. The worst years of my life, she said. The language of those classes was just hideous. It could make your skin crawl. The sketches she was doing in the museum were the beginning of something new. Her husband had quietly cleared out the spare bedroom for her and turned it into a sort of a studio. I don't have time to paint often, she said, but I squeeze some in now and then. Kevin even set up two small easels so the girls can join me.

They looked out at the cascading fountain that moved through a wedge in the ceiling above, an inversion of the large, pyramidal skylights jutting up above street level. A drawing class was gathered around a heap of Styrofoam cups on a nearby table. You must think I'm a little weird, Naomi said, pouring myself out like this to you. Not at all, he said. He admired her courage, her openness. I used to be suspicious of people who did this kind of thing, who were too free with the sordid details of their lives, but lately, she went on, in the past few months, I've realized I don't have time to bottle anything up. None of us do, actually. That sort of quiet is toxic, and in my state I have no patience for poison.

Eventually her cellphone rang and she walked away to answer it. When she returned she apologized but said she had to be going. He stood to say goodbye and for some reason he hugged her, as though he had known her for more than an hour. He worried he had crossed a boundary he shouldn't have, but she must have sensed his unease because she almost immediately thanked him. They exchanged emails and she began walking back toward the main building. He headed for the contemporary wing and was already some distance from the waterfall when he felt a hand on his arm. It was Naomi, out of breath. For you, she said, handing him her sketch of Sargent's painting. He told her he couldn't possibly, but she would have none of it. She just smiled her direct yet enigmatic smile and thanked him again for lunch. Then she put her hand on his cheek, pulled his face toward hers. It was a short, soft kiss, full of sadness and, he thought later, lust, but then her face drained of its emotion and she turned to leave once more. As she rushed down the hallway, maybe to meet her husband, he looked both at her receding figure and that of the reclining one in the drawing. He sought to name the similarity between her and the woman in Sargent's painting, Rose-Marie. It wasn't nonchalance, he knew that much by now, and he could only hope it wasn't that the woman in front of him would also die young.

By the time he reached the museum's east building, his nerves were too frayed to do anything other than drift through the architecture. He wondered if the whole exchange hadn't been a dream, an effect of the slight hangover still enveloping him. He watched the same guards from a dozen different vantages in the building's central atrium, and each time they seemed physically altered, as though they had actually changed. In a ground-floor gallery, two guards were discussing *The Autobiography of Malcolm X* in front of Jackson Pollock's *Number 1, 1950*. The older guard asked the younger one if he knew it, but the younger one said he liked graphic novels. Comic books? the older guard asked. Nah, man, the other said. They're better than that. The older guard then explained why Malcolm had been as important as he was, but that, and this he said in a whisper, white people were always afraid of him. Still are, he said. The Panthers, too. For his part, he had, unlike the younger guard, read the *Autobiography* and he loved its mix of spleen and self-invention, so as he sat on the bench in front of Pollock's painting, he wanted nothing more than to join their conversation but couldn't work up the courage. Maybe it was a result of the conversation (the older guard was now outlining the similarities, in the end, between Malcolm and Dr. King), but he could no longer connect Pollock's work to the action that had always been its prime virtue. He worried, as he looked around the room, that the same fate would befall other painters he had long admired: Mark Rothko, Agnes Martin, Jasper Johns. He worried that all the art he loved, like all the people he loved, would one day lose the power to move him, if it hadn't already—that these works would become little more than historical curiosities, requiring heaps of context to resuscitate them, however briefly. Staring deeper into the canvas, he struggled to link his affection to its objects. What was it in a person that moved another? And did the reasons really matter? He wanted to believe that naming them wouldn't make any difference, but he also worried, scrutinizing Pollock's drips and splatters, that his feelings were failing him.

He left the museum in a state of near-panic. He had spent too long at the gallery and would now have to rush back to the hotel, change quickly, then leave again for the conference. Given the brief amount of time he was to speak, the amount of trouble he had gone through first to write the text then to travel here to present it seemed excessive. He slumped into the back of a taxi and gave the driver the name of his hotel back in Crystal City. Once in his room, he changed shirts and put on a sport coat, grabbed the scarf his wife had packed after checking the weather the morning before. It was an unusual flourish for him, red scarf wrapped rakishly around his neck, waiting there in the hotel lobby for another taxi to pull up in the drizzle. He hadn't read over his text aloud, but rather than do so with the driver listening he watched the signs pass by for Pentagon City, the Kennedy Center, and the National Zoo.

After the formalities at the registration desk, he found the room easily, and with a half-hour to spare he went to the hotel bar and downed a whiskey and ginger. He had no idea what kind of audience to expect, and although Marc, the graduate student who had invited him, had told him the names of the other panelists, he had forgotten all but one. He looked through his program—the same program he saw on tables all around him—and read through the list of names. Other than himself and two people whose work he hadn't read, there was a young superstar on the panel who was certain to draw a small crowd. As it neared the top of the hour, the people in the bar began to clear out, only to be replenished by others coming from sessions that were just ending. He walked back to the conference room.

Marc greeted him warmly and introduced the other panelists. The superstar was a tall man who unnecessarily leaned down to shake his hand before rolling back on his heels and scanning the room. The second panelist was a man from Lincoln, Nebraska, shy and unassuming, his limbs lanky and his hair beginning to recede. He had written a book of poems that interrogated the work of Gerard Manley Hopkins, or so he learned from the back cover of the copy the man gave him. The lone woman in the group was fifty-ish with a mousey face and glasses that were nearly too large. She would be speaking, she told him, about the work of a few African-American women. In particular, she planned to speak about a poet who, he gathered, would be in the audience that day.

Before long, Marc was talking into the microphone, introducing the panelists and their theme, interruption. The superstar, who had briefly sauntered off, rushed over to his seat, as though he had, until now, been oblivious to the proceedings. Consciously or not, he had timed his entrance to Marc's description of his books to date, each of which seemed to have won an award. The introduction was littered with so many quotes from well-known writers that it occurred to him, as Marc spoke—though he was immediately ashamed of it—that perhaps Marc had organized the panel with the primary goal of meeting, and ingratiating himself to, the superstar, but soon the Hopkins poet (for how else was one to think of him?) started to speak and he shook off any ill will. The man began with a cursory explanation of Hopkins's sprung rhythm, which he read primarily as an interruption—not an elaboration, he emphasized—of traditional metrical patterns. He then outlined how much of what had become known as twentieth-century experimentalism was in many ways a version of Hopkins's interruption. He spoke at length about Ronald Johnson's erasure of *Paradise Lost* before concluding that the only strategy that made sense any longer was to interrupt the interruption: to compose the text suggested by Johnson's erasure, for example. This would not result in a preponderance of Pierre Menards, he insisted, referring to Borges's story in which a Frenchman rewrites *Don Quixote* without either remembering or copying it. Instead, the Hopkins poet seemed to be suggesting that everyone write new versions of *Paradise Lost*, that the models tradition provided were endlessly generative, and not just for ironic purposes. The canon could be restorative, too. But by then he had become needlessly distracted by the superstar who, leaning back in his chair next to him, was thoughtfully stroking his bushy beard.

Next, the woman on the panel spoke. Her voice was large and more compelling than he would have expected. His attention wandered, however. He looked out at the roughly forty people in the room, only two of whom were black, one the woman whose work was being discussed. When he tuned back in, he could tell the presentation was smart, but it elided the question of the poet's race, and to him this suddenly seemed not an act of informed restraint but of cowardice, the same cowardice that had overtaken him that morning in the museum. He knew the poet's work she was discussing, and it was saturated with complex questions about identity. He realized in that moment that white people, himself included, were always doing what the woman at the table was doing: to not speak about difference was a privilege he had so internalized that he failed to recognize its effects. What lay behind the woman's smart presentation was the assumption that white was the default color, which could only mean that she did not need to justify her relationship, as a white woman, to the work of a black writer, but that the work of the black writer had to justify itself, formally and thematically, to the white culture into which it had entered and, in essence, interrupted. He began to feel his blood boil. The panel had been a mistake. He should have skipped it entirely, spent the afternoon in the museum—or with Naomi, maybe, back at his hotel. Why, he asked himself, did writers convene in this way to begin with? What was to be gained through these public displays of private ruminations? But before he had time to come up with any kind of answer, the audience was applauding the woman's presentation and Marc was calling his name.

Near the start of Hou Hsiao-Hsien's 2007 movie *Flight of the Red Balloon*, he began, a middle-aged woman wearing a white coat and gold scarf finds herself in the middle of the shot. She is, apparently, neither cast nor crew. Curious, she pauses at the street corner, looks directly at the camera, then hurries on. Her gaze—which could be directed at any *you* seated in the theater or happily propped up in bed—cuts through the film. But if you didn't know to look for her, you might not catch her. I only noticed her, he said, the second time around.

There are a few more such moments in the film. Not long after the first, a Scandinavian-looking woman with red hair down to her waist, wearing a pink and mauve sweater, walks through the shot. Her gaze lasts only a second, but the quiet shock of it is enough to jolt you out of whatever experience you were having. What fascinates me is this: Hou could have filtered these interruptions out. He could have had the Paris police block off the streets. He could have cordoned off his art. But in allowing these women to walk across the scene, in inviting them—inviting anyone—to interrupt the shot, Hou calls the viewer's attention to the fact that this film, which is obsessed with the parallel play of disparate worlds (a child's and an adult's), is not life. It's as if someone were holding up a placard reminding us that the world of the film is not the world, that realism is not reality. But even as it simulates, the film creates, producing both the illusion of reality and a distinct reality of its own. Two worlds occupy the same space concurrently, and what we witness in the women is the allowance for that difference. At any given moment we are both inside of, and removed from, the world.

He paused for thirty seconds, as he had privately advised Marc he would, before beginning again. In the original version of *Flight of the Red Balloon*, he continued, Albert Lamorisse's 1956 short *Le Ballon Rouge*, a young boy follows and is followed by a red balloon through the streets of Paris. We watch the balloon move along sidewalks, through windows and doors; it crosses over walls and roofs. At one point the balloon waits for the boy outside his school. In the opening shot of Hou Hsiao-Hsien's film, a small boy stands outside a Metro station looking up at a red balloon caught in a tree, begging the balloon to come with him. He offers it a hundred candies, two million caramels, but the balloon does not appear to be listening. Until, that is, it starts following the path of the train on which the boy, Simon, is riding; later, it shows up in the window of the small apartment he shares with his mother (where it seems to be trying to push its way in) and in a large mural he passes on his walk home from school. His Taiwanese nanny, Song, is making a film about red balloons, and in the final scene of the movie, while Simon's class discusses Felix Vallotton's 1899 painting *Le Ballon*, a red balloon appears in the skylight in the Musée d'Orsay. In the painting, a young child runs after a red balloon drifting along in the sunlight; in the distance, two adults—the child's parents, perhaps—are ensconced in deep shadows cast by tall trees, indifferent to the child playing in the foreground. These same shadows seem to grasp at the child, who, as though sensing the danger of a darkening world, barely escapes their clutches as he moves in the direction of the balloon. While the children continue to talk about the painting, the camera cuts to a shot of Simon's balloon floating impassively over the rooftops of Paris. The movie ends.

Another pause. Someone was having (or staging) a coughing fit, and the door shut loudly behind them. The mother and son at the center of the film, he said, move through their scenes separated by an almost tangible veil of mutual incomprehension. They ask each other in turn, *Are you okay?*—little knowing what that might mean for the other. The child—whose t-shirt reads *Change the World*—occupies a reality fully removed from that of his mother, the hectic pace of whose life would be unnerving were it not for the quiet, playful scenes the son carves out around her. These two realities coexist: the world of the mother, who happens to be a puppeteer, and the world of the child, in which everything is potentially a puppet—a plaything, a toy. The film's unrelenting melancholy is born of the fact that we know the child will lose his childhood. Later he will only be able to attempt to regain it—perhaps, like his mother, through art. For the adults in the film the spirit of childhood is both a distant memory and a vicarious pleasure. Hou suggests that it's the tension between work and play, between our real and imagined worlds, that animates both. Art is not life, nor life art, though each must allow for the other, providing a space in which to embrace mundane and even violent interruptions. A shout. A balloon. A woman who pauses before the camera then quickly hurries away.

The second hand on his watch made its slow half-orbit around the clock face. For Emmanuel Levinas, he continued, the question isn't whether being is, but how it situates itself—and in relation to whom or to what. If he's right, then the work of art poses another question: how does art relate to the spaces it inhabits and the persons with whom it interacts? How does writing—no, how does a writer uncover himself? How does he reveal his face? Interruption is a way to offer what the poet George Oppen also wants: not truth, but each other—that the other sees our face and we theirs. Inasmuch as interruption involves, as Levinas says, the risky uncovering of oneself, in sincerity, the breaking up of inwardness and the abandon of all shelter, exposure to traumas, and vulnerability, the woman walking through the shot at the film's beginning is a breakthrough. One sees her face, but beneath it discerns another: a different, albeit overlapping, reality turns to look our way. Two friends have a conversation in a café—a child interjects. In the middle of the play, an intermission. In the middle of the show, a commercial. Even the eye interrupts itself: to see an object properly the eye looks away from it, only to look back again.

He couldn't tell whether, given the blank stares from some audience members, he needed to prepare himself for the pillory. My wife finds the film soothing, he said. Something about the light, detached quality of the lives led by Simon and his nanny. The mother, Suzanne, is entangled in the lives around her, but Simon and Song drift peacefully through the film, much like the red balloon above them. The question for me is how to live like this, or how to write from the space Hou describes, where childhood is conflated with something almost Taoist. A dispassionate participant, free from the chords that tether others. The puppet show Suzanne is mounting in the film is a strange one: a version of an old Chinese legend in which a scholar, Zhang, must boil the sea, ladle by ladle, in order to force the Dragon King to leave his home in the depths. Only by so doing can Zhang convince the Dragon King to let him marry his daughter. Zhang is aided in his efforts by a goddess who gives him two gold coins that, when placed in his pot, will make the sea boil more rapidly. This may be as fine a criterion as any: you would boil the sea for those you love. But the version of the world in which the sea is too limitless to boil is only one version. There may be more alluring stories to live by. For a puppet, anyway, the string is not a bind but its inverse. Each line is a hallway at the end of which lies something like freedom. The puppet suggests that the entanglements of our lives might also be vehicles for liberation.

And yet, he went on, one still from the film shows a man dressed in green and following Simon with a large pole, on the end of which is, presumably, the balloon, out of frame. Song tells Suzanne, regarding her own film, that green is one color that can be digitally erased without much trouble. The man, she continues, will disappear when she edits her film, and the balloon will appear to be untethered. Its freedom is a special effect and Hou wants us to recognize it as such. Or rather, he wants us simultaneously to admire this freedom and accept its artificiality, what W.G. Sebald called the effect of the real.

He was starting to drift from aesthetics. The cougher had come back into the room, but seemed on the verge of leaving it once more. Someone's cellphone played the opening bars of a Latin dance song. He knew this turn had been coming from the first sentence, but now, reading these final sections aloud, he had trouble getting through them, saturated as they were with his own dilemmas. Throughout the film, he read, Simon's father, Pierre, is conspicuously absent. We learn that he is in Montreal, writing a book. He's been gone for two years, and in a particularly mean-spirited exchange Suzanne's downstairs tenant tells her Pierre's never coming back. That much is obvious without anyone having to say it. The hole in Suzanne's life is visible on screen, and though she attributes it to her difficult situation, to the fact that grown-ups are complicated, at one point she simply says to Pierre over the phone, I need a man by my side. It's less obvious whether Simon needs one, but it may be that he is still too young for any real holes in his life to have developed, or that one definition of childhood has to do with a certain imperviousness to the contours of one's own psychology. Each of us must traverse the shadows our parents cast over our lives, and at some point in his fictional future, Simon will have to make sense of his father's absence, which hangs heavily, though irregularly, over the film.

As I continue to write, he read, I become less and less certain about which text I am writing, much as in watching *Flight of the Red Balloon* I'm never quite sure which film I'm seeing. Is this a version of Lamorrise's earlier film or something else entirely? It's even more difficult to divide Hou's film from Song's film within it. This film within a film also stars Simon, and when at one point we see a piece of it playing on Song's laptop, the scene is unmistakably the one from the beginning of Hou's film. Where one ends and the other begins is anyone's guess. Hou may be making a point here about the architecture of reality, both in life and in art (if that distinction still makes any sense)—that it's foolish to insist on autonomy. To say, at any given time, that we are experiencing one thing and not another, that the reality we encounter is such and not so. For even if the seams are visible, what use would there be in pulling the stitches apart?

A final pause—filled with his own tension, if no one else's—and then the punchline:

Does it seem like a happy picture or a sad one? Simon's teacher asks as they talk about Vallotton's painting.

A happy one, a student immediately responds.

It's a bit happy and a bit sad, says another.

And why is that? asks the teacher.

Because one part is dark and there's sunlight in the other part, says the student.

That's right, says the teacher. The child is in the sunlight.


He closed the folder and leaned back in his chair. Much of what followed, in the superstar's presentation, was highly ironic and drew hearty laughter from the audience. It felt as if the room was his, that it had been from the beginning. The superstar argued, as far as he could tell, that sometimes a person just wants a cookie, and that it is this kind of interruption literature can best provide. In the short Q&A that followed, most comments were for the other presenters, but at the end an older man rose to ask him a question. Considering the other papers read today, in which certain proposals for action were either stated outright or strongly implied, he said, your talk stands out to me as—forgive me for saying so—somewhat lacking in substance. You generalize about childhood and about interruption, couched of course in the discussion of this elegant film, but what are you saying? It seems that if you are arguing for anything in your presentation, it's this wishy-washy relationship with reality, or the passive, uncritical stance embodied in these, well, let's call them dramatic pauses. Is writing just a passive performance? Does it matter if the performance is about anything? He could sense, as the man spoke, a certain air of approval in the room, and so he was surprised when, before he had a chance to speak, the superstar came to his defense. I thought it was a wonderful talk myself, he said, and it captured for me exactly the kind of interruption I was thinking about in my own presentation, albeit in a different direction.

He took a deep breath and said that the man wasn't entirely wrong in his criticism. While he disagreed, obviously, with the assertion that the talk had been without content, while he disagreed with the accusation that his approach had been uncritical, he believed the man hit the nail on the head when he spoke of passivity. I have no interest, he said, in creating proposals for action, as you put it. My feeling is there have been many such proposals, and they often obscure the real business of living one's life and writing one's work. Manifestos never move us into the light, he said. They only keep us in the dark. The man visibly shrugged before he sat down. Marc thanked the audience and the panelists, and people began to file out. The superstar leaned toward him to say that he meant what he had said. He thought it had been a lovely talk and, handing him a card, wondered whether he might send him a copy. Then, after complimenting the other speakers, the superstar again sauntered off. The remaining panelists asked whether he wanted to join them for dinner, but he was tired, he said, which was at least half-true.

As he made his way toward the lobby he saw, sitting alone on an armchair in a quiet stretch of the otherwise crowded hallway, the poet who had been the subject of one of the presentations. She wore her hair in long, graying dreadlocks pulled back behind her head, and her dress was something out of Mao's China. She met his gaze and held it, and he had an intense feeling of recognition: that this woman knew him and that he should know her. He walked up and introduced himself. I know who you are, she said, laughing. Have a seat. He collapsed in the armchair next to hers, both of which, bolted to the floor, angled toward the same point in the middle of the hall. These things exhaust me, too, she said, as though reading the look on his face, but I enjoyed your talk. The gods I most identify with are household ones. What had she thought of the discussion of her work, he asked, but she only smiled and said it had been, she paused to look for the right word, engaging. He wanted to say then what he had thought in the panel, that the talk had ignored important parts of her writing. Instead he said something about the drizzle. She nodded and smiled once more. There was a quiet in her he found both comforting and unsettling. She seemed to say no more than necessary, and was willing to let him stumble through the gaps, which he did again and again, asking her at one point how long she would be staying in DC. I live here, she said, laughing again. He apologized. How would you have known where I live, she asked. She hesitated for a moment, looking up at the ceiling tiles for guidance. Then she leaned forward in her chair, suddenly serious. Is there something you want to say to me, sweetie?

A few people rushed past, late for whatever event they were attending. Music was streaming quietly through hidden speakers—a ukulele version, he couldn't help but notice, of "Somewhere Over the Rainbow." He thought back to that moment in front of Pollock's painting, and suddenly it came over him in a rush, as though the pressure had been building all day—or longer than that, really, maybe for months or even years. There was a lot he wanted to say to her, to Naomi, to his wife. They moved him, these women—to reciprocity, and to care. He wanted to make that clear. Wanted to make up for the times it hadn't been, either to himself or to others. And yet he felt so acutely just then the impossibility of the space between them, the difficulty of saying anything to the poet across from him, a woman whose life, like Naomi's, he had little access to, or purchase on. But he had seen something in her eyes, had he not? She had recognized him for who he was, had seen not through him, but through *to* him, as though cutting away all the protective layers he had cultivated, all the posturing and posing, between himself and the world.

That woman's talk, he said finally. It was bullshit. It was, she said, nodding. They both looked out into that space between them, as though weighing it, measuring what it meant. But it doesn't really change anything, does it? he asked. Not a thing, she said. And then he remembered, though he couldn't quite say from where, that it was necessary to hold onto what mattered. The poet mattered. Naomi mattered. His wife and son mattered. But the panel didn't matter. Superstardom didn't matter, though divorced from it the superstar did matter. And do I, he wondered. Do I matter? he said aloud. She looked askance at him for a moment, as though he had propositioned her in a language he didn't fully understand. And from then on, until he stood up, wished her a good evening, and continued walking to the lobby, there was only that space again, which seemed neither to expand nor contract, but to remain, almost like a vacuum, as invisible forces now pulled them together, now pushed them apart.

## 5

Around the turn of the sixth century, a man named Liu Xie published what is widely considered to be the first book of literary criticism in China. Entitled *The Literary Imagination and the Carving of Dragons* (*Wenxin diaolong*), the book was likely composed during Liu's ten-year residency at the Dinglin Temple outside modern-day Nanjing. A somewhat conservative critic, Liu promoted innovation based on the classics and was clearly anxious about what he saw as increasing ornamentation in literary works. Attempts at articulating a consistent structure to his theories have largely been in vain, however, as the book contains any number of glaring discrepancies and self-contradictions.

Beyond his contribution to Chinese literature, not much is known about Liu's life. It seems his family's fortunes widely fluctuated over time, and his most immediate ancestors were legendary eccentrics, including one man with a penchant for eating scabs: visitors were often obliged to give him their own. Straitened circumstances required that Liu develop a certain industriousness, and when his book failed to move its initial readers, he decided to show the manuscript to Shen Yue, the unparalleled literary master of his time. It wasn't as easy, apparently, as sending him the manuscript attached to an email, so Liu posed as a bookseller and waited for Shen outside his home. Shen bought the book, read it, and found it remarkable enough to keep on his desk from that day forward. Liu subsequently held a series of government posts without ever ascending to any real power or prominence. Near the end of his life, back at Dinglin Temple, he became a monk, but before he had the formal opportunity to take his vows, which meant shaving his hair and beard, he burned them off instead, just to prove his determination. He died within a year of his conversion.

In the twenty-eighth of fifty chapters in his *Wenxin diaolong*, Eliot Weinberger explains, Liu investigates the mysterious conjunction of wind and bone. To express emotions, Weinberger writes, one must begin with wind; to organize words, one must have bone. He whose bone structure is well exercised will be well versed in rhetoric; he who is deep of wind will articulate well his feelings. It would seem, he continues, that wind is sentiment and ideas, and bone is language, but Liu also says that to be thin in ideas and fat in words, confused and disorganized, is to lack bone. And yet when ideas are incomplete, lifeless and without vitality, it is also to lack wind. What is wind and what is bone have never been conclusively determined by subsequent generations of Chinese critics, but what is certain, according to Weinberger's reading, is that the perfect balance of wind and bone, the metaphor for the ideal poem, is a bird.

That June, I became embroiled in a feud between writers, brought about by the mysterious firing of a divisive poet but beloved teacher. Another poet had assumed a position of relative power and had, some said, decided the first poet was an obstacle, or competitor, to be removed. This had unleashed a backlash from the first poet's students and friends, who began organizing to remove the second poet from her job at the university, then in the middle of a downsizing in which others—administrators and adjuncts, mostly—were losing their livelihoods. It was a virtual war conducted over email and social media, and yet how one situated oneself in the argument had physical effects, determining which parties one was invited to, which cafés one frequented, even which readings one might comfortably attend.

The feud spilled into my lap when the first poet, a single mother with whom I had often commiserated about parenting, mentioned me in a lengthy email denouncing the second poet, who had so avoided the entanglements of family that she, unlike me, had become a veritable poetry machine, churning out book after book. Originally the email had been sent to the administration only, but soon the first poet was forwarding it to everyone she knew. I had information, she had written, regarding the second poet's job performance, since our offices had been, around the time my son was born, ostensibly across the hall from one another. The first poet's claim was true enough: in nearly two years, I had rarely seen the second poet. Even during her posted hours her door was shut, and when mine was open I frequently fielded complaints and queries from irritated students. It was enough of a problem that I had privately expressed my concerns, in my last semester as an employee, to our department chair, a third poet whose ineffectual leadership was equally to blame for the first poet's dismissal, if not more so, though no one said this at the time. That the third poet never responded to email, for instance, seemed to be a matter of principle, although I never learned which one. She was, thankfully, more diligent about returning phone calls, but by far the best way to get in touch with her was to listen for her footfalls on the stairs then barge into her office. Our conversation about the second poet months earlier, which had taken place under such improvised circumstances, had been brief and collegial, and I left her tiny, disheveled office, overflowing with piles of papers and books, both with a clear conscience and a feeling that nothing would be done.

My response to the emails that emerged from the first poet's claims was consistent and a cop-out. I wanted no part of the campaign against the second poet, I wrote, though I freely acknowledged, as I had to the chair, that her absenteeism was unethical, a claim that was not only at odds with my refusal to join the effort but amounted, as I see now, to a de facto endorsement of it. And yet whether the second poet kept regular work hours was not really my concern, or so I felt, nor was the first poet's objective as noble as she framed it: that her justifiable anger at the loss of her livelihood was now taking the shape of a public project to save the culture of the school struck me as disingenuous. Whatever else the feud was about, it was also an economic crisis, a matter of resources. To chalk it up to bad blood, even if this played a role, was to ignore the painful gap, which I was then navigating, between the expanding supply of poets and the dwindling demand for us in the academic institutions where we sought work. It was to ignore the way scarcity breeds factions and how, once this happens, there is often little room for escape.

And so as one screed after another arrived in my inbox, I turned—either as a diversion or a consolation, I didn't know—to my consideration of

Liu's ancient text. This is a reason to write in notebooks, I thought, ignoring the latest run of inflammatory messages: the temptation to distraction is just too great on the internet, that information monster that took the shape, in my imagination, not of a dragon but of an ineffable sea creature. Liu Xie's problem was not so different. His anxiety about privileging style over substance may be a reasonable analog for a world that favors knowing over thinking or, for that matter, feeling. Still, there was something to be said about instant access to the biography of a 1,500-year-old critic and the availability, seconds later, of its author's email address on the Harvard website.

In her response, the sinologist explained that in ancient China dragons weren't exactly mythical. The taxonomists of the time considered them insects, albeit of the highest order, and in fact carving dragons replaced a more derogatory term, carving insects, which was a way of calling writing a trivial occupation. She wrote that Liu's work was indeed the first of its kind in China but that its importance had been exaggerated. When, under Western influence, Chinese scholars and writers in the early twentieth century came to believe in the supreme value of a systematic theoretical treatise on literature, something in the vein of Aristotle's *Poetics*, they turned to Liu Xie. The majority of classical Chinese literary theory and criticism, she continued, was never in such a form but rather existed in prefaces, colophons, letters, and more importantly, remarks on poetry (*shi hua*).

Liu Xie was part of a tradition, she went on, in which language more often obstructs than assists communication: it is a suggestive aid, to be discarded when truth is attained. Words decay, after all, and why shouldn't they? Meanings that might once have been obvious—the meaning, say, of carving insects—come to require exegesis. Household names become strange, and, as in a horror film, words start losing limbs or stagger around like zombies. And sometimes it happens, I thought, that words take on meanings their authors never could have imagined. Keats couldn't have known that, two hundred years after he wrote his famous ode to a nightingale, scientists would discover that the plaintive anthem had increased in volume to overcome the din of passing cars, and that the bird is sophisticated enough to sing more loudly on weekday mornings than on the weekend. Nor could Liu Xie have anticipated that one day that summer, on the shoulder of the highway, I would see a small hawk that had been struck by a car not long before. Liu could not have imagined the kind of world that could so mutilate his metaphor. Nor, obviously, could he have pictured the cardboard box into which I poked a series of holes before transporting the injured bird, with my son in tow, to a shelter some twenty minutes away. I hadn't known about these refuges for maimed owls, hawks, and eagles that, because of their injuries, cannot be released back into the wild, nor had I imagined how affected I would be at the sight of a magnificent barred owl missing its right eye. Spacious as its enclosure was, I could not adjust to its one-eyed gaze. The hawk survived, but its left wing was so severely damaged, the caretakers told me, that it, too, would have to remain in the refuge, where it may still be staring out at its benefactors with a mixture of disinterest and disdain.

In early July, in part to escape the ongoing poetry war, which would soon jump the virtual firebreak into social media, I returned to the mountains, more than six months after I'd last set foot in them. The Forest Service trail leading to the continental divide was easy to find, but hiking up was tough going, and after climbing nearly a thousand feet my legs and head were throbbing. I sat on a large rock facing east and looked out at the long grooves in the hillsides where water gathered and ran downstream. I took a small jar out of my backpack and placed it in an inconspicuous hollow on the far side of the rock. Over the course of the next several hours, as I hiked up and down the trail, I deposited the dozen or so remaining jars I had with me in trees, in streams, in freshly dug holes in the ground. I had been unable to resist the temptation of leaving one on the rugged bench fashioned out of slabs of rock at the top of the trail. I relished the thought of some hiker from the suburbs, some refraction of me, sitting down for the view and discovering the shard of a poem I had left behind. I imagined their bewilderment, which would only be the extension of my own.

If I lingered on the trail that morning, I did so out of the realization that lately there had been few mornings like this one. A good three years had passed since my wife and I had last gone for a hike together, which had been a regular, even weekly, part of our lives prior to becoming parents. That last hike had happened in late April or early May. She was pregnant at the time, and we took a trail that followed a creek into the foothills. The route alternated between long, dry stretches and the most abysmal mud, so thick in places that the only option was to walk through the rushes lining the creek. The mud disappeared as we climbed higher, and though the air was cold we found a sunny rock on the side of the canyon where we ate granola bars and talked about the future. What sort of parents would we be, we wondered. What mistakes could we avoid making?

On the way back down the mountain that morning, having jettisoned my jars, I wondered whether I hadn't been trying to convince myself that I was the kind of person I had once wanted to be instead of the person I was. But if I had never quite become who I set out to be, who exactly was clambering his way down the rocky slope? It was fitting that the boots on my feet were relics from that earlier part of my life during which I not only wrote reams of poetry, much of it execrable stuff, but also spent a fair amount of time outdoors, sometimes with a friend who I later suspected, after we had drifted apart, of having joined the CIA. He was fond of drawing hard lines, and the edges in his poems reflected those in his person. He hated my self-doubt and wouldn't, he said, *pander down* to it. Of course, I could see now how little self-doubt possessed me then and how much, in the years since, it had overtaken me—to the extent that I often felt paralyzed, unable to write another word out of fear that there could be no way to avoid compromising myself, exposing myself as the fraud I thought I was. I had become a kind of anti-poet, and yet the boots I bought for nearly two hundred dollars in 1997 were still, in 2011, remarkably sturdy. Whereas I had grown unrecognizable to myself, the boots were a little worn but otherwise undiminished from their original condition.

Driving home that day, first through Nederland then down through Boulder Canyon, I thought again of Thoreau, who begins his final book, *Faith in a Seed*, with a line from Pliny: trees that do not seed or bear fruit are sinister and inauspicious. I had likewise set for myself the question of dispersal: if a poem is primarily a conveyance—no matter the ways and means by which it conveys—what was I interested in transporting, and to where, or to whom? What could it mean to produce a text that floated down a stream like an acorn? Other animals would never have conceived such a ludicrous project, but surely squirrels store nuts in the ground for the winter, and who's to say my poems, encased in their tiny jars, weren't seeds fallen from a more human tree?

The poetry war reached a fever pitch just after my thirty-second birthday, in early August. A fourth poet, the woman I had met six months earlier in DC, intervened in the exchanges, arguing forcefully, via posts on her Facebook page, against the online campaign. How or why she had become involved sort of baffled me, but I suspected that at some point she had been approached as an outside expert. If so, the effort had backfired. The whole thing was toxic, the fourth poet wrote, and she pleaded with the discontented parties to desist. Nothing good could come of it, she said, but her posts only brought angry reprisals from the first poet and her supporters, who complained in the comment stream that the fourth poet was stifling debate. I am sorry, the fourth poet responded, in what was clearly an address to the first, that you are in such pain, but please remember that the most important thing is to write. This was followed by a flurry of blanket denunciations, public shaming, and vindictive unfriending the likes of which, though new at the time, has since become all too familiar.

Though given the context I might just as easily have adopted it as a rallying cry, the fourth poet's exhortation troubled me. Was writing really more important than the people who produced it? *No people, no significance*, I remembered from Annie Dillard, but I thought maybe the fourth poet had reversed the phrase, that in her formulation the writer's prerogative took precedence, which may be the way most writers conduct their lives, including me, but I was starting to have reservations about such selfishness. The fourth poet seemed to be enthroning a form of egomania, but she had maybe arrived at the conclusion by faulty premises: if people are in pain, they're likely to lash out; therefore, the most important thing is to write. The leap in logic almost elided the pain, even though that probably hadn't been her intention. She had meant for writing to be a balm, I imagine, but what was it supposed to heal, and how? That didn't seem to be its purpose, exactly, and though the wounds of plenty of writers made their impressions on the work, if ever someone had been cured by putting pen to paper, or fingers to keyboard, I was, at the time, unaware of it.

I said none of this to the fourth poet, as I was already on unsteady ground, navigating the terra incognita of other people's anxieties. Ever mindful of my reputation—and of the fact that I, like the first poet, was subject to sudden dismissal, even at my new institution—I privately applauded, in a personal email, the fourth poet's courage, but also restated my refusal to get involved, a position I increasingly understood as cowardly, considering that while I didn't want to be implicated, by virtue of my unwilling but ongoing inclusion in, for example, the address lines of various email threads, I was. I could see there was something amiss in my response, but I couldn't figure out where I was going wrong.


Meanwhile, I slowly littered poems across the Front Range. I had worked for years on the manuscript, *That Honorary Coxswain of the Heart*, from which the fragments in the jars derived. I either couldn't let it be or it wouldn't let me go. In the beginning, I had written in a purple notebook consisting of 150 9.5" x 6" college-ruled sheets, a notebook that also contained addresses, phone numbers, lists of words, course schedules, names of hotels in Seville, Granada, and Cold-Spring-on-Hudson, as well as meeting minutes, train schedules, film times, love letters, book lists, collaborations, and lines culled from writers I was then reading. The following, for instance: *If your nerve deny you— / Go above your nerve* (Emily Dickinson), *My tongue is a curve in the ear. Vision is lies.* (Basil Bunting). The earliest use of the notebook was probably sometime in August of 2004, the latest was little more than a year later, and in an entry dated 3/14/05, I found the first version of the phrase that would become the book's title:

By that logic even the most insane of Jesus's preachers would check the tickers. Trade the trucks for a more modest sense of sponsorship. A larger collar or longer health food store. All media amass at the edges of the communiqués. And so God bless your layers, loser. Your mother senses a whole. Plastic motif of iris, daisy. On so much used-to-be, once-was. By which I designate decorum déclassé. And for that, I'm sorry—sorry it didn't, I mean, work out as you'd intended. Some people subsisting, e.g., the honorary coxswain of my heart, a string quartet, you get the picture. Once we grow enough it's possible, in mind, to know even the most abstruse person is a friend, the opening of some piano piece, or the brief musical phrase as it pokes its head just over conversation. I was the first one here by far and I'll tell you not to look, to stare, i.e., to ogle. Once, when this book was smaller, it was filled with ludicrous facts; now it's all pages, leaves in the sense of tickets blowing about the concrete, browned with age. Who's to say we'd rather have time stand still, rather call the miserable situation some other shade of purge. No, I mean there are so many reds & greens & scarves in those colors. We should figure out a team like "hey" and try to catch the wishes.

By the summer of 2011, I found this text almost impenetrable, but if, as Eileen Myles has said, a poem is a way to balance one's inside with one's outside, then you could say that the writings in the notebook— culled from conversations in a bright, airy café—were poems. I sorted and sifted the cadences pushing their way through the speech I heard all around me. The text on the notebook pages, however, did not in the least resemble the one that, after five years and dozens of drafts, I abandoned. That text became in part the condensation of those conversations, but, once gathered, the language took on a life of its own. It produced associations, invited digressions and divergences. *That Honorary Coxswain of the Heart* was never, not even in its earliest drafts, simply a transcription. The language was a riddle that invited solutions—solutions I never found.

If the book began as an act of revelry, it ended in a kind of malaise. Entropy engulfed the poems at a rate as astonishing as the one at which I had written them. Two poems split in half to form a third—the discarded halves tossed into the recycling bin—or three into shards to form a fourth. Each was a hydra. Everywhere I slashed a new fixation emerged. But every line was also a problem, and I tinkered the book into oblivion. Thousands of lines of verse became little more than a handful on each page; sometimes a single line or couplet scattered over white space was all that remained. On one hand, five years of drafting left me with the marrow, but the poems had also become, to my eyes, hideously deformed. I simultaneously wanted nothing to do with them and thought that if I only rearranged a little more here, pruned a little more there, I would finally have it. Eventually I realized there was no end to the poem. My *Coxswain* seemed destined to call with some regularity, urging me to propel it forward a few more inches. Unless, that is, I was able to come up with some more definitive solution.

Then one day that previous spring I was having lunch with my son, as I sometimes did, at a Mexican place not far from home. The woman at the next table was asking her companion whether he had heard about the local man who inherited a sizable estate from his estranged father, the owner of a string of tire shops in the area. At first, she said, the man was elated. He paid off a few debts. He planned a long trip, bought a new house. And then the shit hit the fan. Everything you could imagine might go wrong did. His wife became violently ill on the trip. She nearly died. The house he had bought was in a dangerous part of the state for wildfires. It burned down. Finally, one of his father's associates came under investigation for racketeering, and the son himself was embroiled in a lengthy lawsuit with the IRS. One day it hit him. Everything had been because of his inheritance. His father had been an unhappy man, a spiteful one, and the son became convinced that he had put some sort of curse on the money. He decided to get rid of what remained. First, he tried donating lump sums to charities, but the charities, because of his legal situation, didn't want a dime. He offered it to family members, but there, too, for a variety of reasons, he made little headway. After several months, he began disposing of the cash in tiny parcels. Some he left in public bathrooms or in rest areas. He threw neatly bagged bundles out his window as he drove down the highway. Two boys found $5,000 along the side of a creek. A single mother of four found three grand on her lawn one morning when she went to get the paper. Sometimes it seemed he even had a sense of humor about it. A retired man browsing the mysteries in a used bookstore, for example, found a wad of crisp $100 bills behind a book whose plot revolved around a complicated scheme for extortion. The police only figured out who was responsible when a carefully hidden squad car saw a small package fly out of the driver's side of a silver pickup speeding down a country road late at night.

By then my son was getting bored with the restaurant, so we had to leave before the woman finished her story, but the first thing I did when we got home, after putting my son down for his nap, was to print out what remained of *That Honorary Coxswain of the Heart*. Now how to finish the job? Disposing of it in a single shot seemed a little discourteous. Pert, even. Renunciation can also be a feast, even for an anti-poet. For several days I cast about for an answer, and then I came across a box of old jars in the garage. They were of a uniform size and shape—baby food jars I had kept for some reason. I immediately remembered my grandmother, my mother's mother: how she prepared her preserves, setting each jar on the table when she was finished with it, until they had grown into quite an orderly collection. I must, I thought, put my poems in these jars.


By the time a fifth poet became involved, I sensed the crisis was having an effect on my longstanding friendship with a sixth poet, whom I now suspected of pulling away, in large part because of how I had isolated myself in the scandal, neither staying out of it entirely, as I had so often claimed, nor throwing in my lot with the people who mattered.

But that was just the trouble: I couldn't tell who mattered, nor seem to remember that everyone did. I'd lost that ability, ironically enough, by writing poems. My whole way of being, which extended to stuffing my poems in jars, was too self-involved for allegiance.

True, I distrusted the second poet, saw her as an unscrupulous climber, but on the other hand, the first poet—as painful as her situation might have been—seemed to be externalizing her grief onto the allies she recruited, her anger onto the enemies she made. This realization simultaneously garnered my sympathy and drove me away, not toward the second poet's position but perhaps, insomuch as she had decried the whole thing as ruinous, toward the fourth's. At the same time, the fourth poet's insistence that writing mattered more than people, although it had been my default position for years, undercut her objections.

Into this morass the fifth poet took his formidable and character-istically domineering steps. Once he made it known that the second poet had his putatively cautious but ultimately unwavering support, there was only one route the resolution could take: the first poet was effectively censured and banished while the second poet's position solidified. The virtual conglomeration of agitators disbanded, and the fourth poet returned to her brilliant, demanding verse. While their re-lationship had always been warm, if sometimes fraught with tensions I never understood, the fallout between the first and fifth poets was fiery and protracted.

At a garden party that August, for example, a birthday celebration for the sixth poet's son, the fifth poet confronted me: whose side had I been on this whole time? Of course the question itself was absurd, an ironic reflection of the political rhetoric the fifth poet deconstructed in his poems, but once cornered I said, between bites of chocolate cake, that I no longer knew what the dispute was about, that no one seemed capable of sustaining any level of reasonableness or civility. Worse yet, in that the whole community appeared to be actively, aggressively disinterested in these things, I considered everyone involved as guilty as everyone else. There were, the fifth poet told me, endless exchanges between the two of them just then, but I knew as he spoke, seeming to take me into his confidence, that irrevocable damage had been done.

My unwillingness to come out from the shadows had turned me into a ventriloquist's dummy—or, in keeping with a lively scene from the birthday party, a piñata. In muffling my voice, whatever it was it might have said, I had in effect sacrificed myself, and as my wife and I left the party with our son that day, I could see that in the coming years perhaps only the fourth poet, a woman I barely knew, would have anything to do with me, a hunch that mostly came true.

By the end of the month, Hurricane Irene was moving up the Atlantic seaboard, drenching everything in its path, the city of Tripoli, in western Libya, was becoming the most dangerous place in the world practically overnight, and the sixth poet, who had stayed out of the fray in enviable ways, was evading my questions about the continuing fallout. Considering how close the fifth and sixth poets were—they had been friends and rivals for thirty years—I had little doubt that my diminished stock in the eyes of the fifth poet was visible in the eyes of the sixth. As I followed the developments in the live blogs tracking the major world events of the moment, as I witnessed history unfolding in the unprecedented ways technology makes possible, I still had no way of knowing, other than by intuition, that in six months it would be three months since I had heard from the sixth poet, that in six more months it would be nine. And finally I saw where I had gone wrong.

As a poet, I had been incapable of saying anything of substance, anything that was not the most derivative kind of abstraction. As Liu Xie might have said, I was all bone, no wind, treating the words I culled from conversations as objects to be moved about on the page as a child might move blocks about on the floor. But words don't really work that way, or rather that's only one part of how they work. They derive their power from another source. And it was this source, whatever it was, wherever it lived, that I had always been looking for but, at least as a poet, had never found. Put another way, I had tried to fend for myself that summer, abstracting myself from the feud, when I should have sought refuge in others, keeping close to the sixth poet as one might a mother, which she had been for me in her way. Because I was more calculating than courageous, more bone than wind, I had been basically abandoned or devoured.

This may be why the wounded hawk haunted my dreams that August, as though it were more than a metaphor, as though there were more meaning in it than meaning could hold. The hawk didn't die, and none of the poets died either, even if Liu Xie had died fifteen centuries ago, and my father's father had shot himself in the basement of his home in suburban Chicago, and my maternal grandfather was nearly dead, having been remanded to one of those places where old folks shuffle back and forth, refusing to give up the ghost, and the strangeness that had pervaded my life, so much of it self-imposed, showed no signs of abating, and I had failed some friends or they had failed me, and soon it would be months since I had written a poem, and then it would be years.

At the end of that difficult summer my friend Naomi sent me, quite out of the blue, a document she had been encouraged to write, during a recent stay in the hospital, by an earnest young woman whose function was unclear to her, but who seemed to be part therapist, part social worker, and part doctor, and who spent most of her time getting patients to write their autobiographies, as though, beaten down by illness, one might take refuge in one's story. Naomi had chosen to write mostly of her disease, which had begun in her right eye several years earlier and which had eventually cost her its use. She described a vision of a poorly picked weed that came to her while she was lying in bed one night, not long after her eye was surgically removed. The leaves were gone, but the roots were growing, and that night I imagined, she wrote, these tangled branches reaching down from my empty eye socket into my left breast. I started to panic. I sat upright in bed and began pulling at my neck, my chest, my face, looking for the spot where I might uproot the curse that was now, I had no doubt, moving through my system. My husband woke and tried to calm me, but I was inconsolable. I finally fell asleep very early in the morning, but the pathways, I knew, were established, and when a couple of years later new tests came back positive I was floored less by the news than by the accuracy of my premonition.

Had it helped? I asked. Had her autobiography healed her in any sense? Had writing, in other words, been the most important thing? She had given a shape to her story, she said, but it was only one of many, no more or less valid than the one she might have found in the perspective of her daughters, or from the point of view of her metastasizing cells. No, writing had not helped her to see what her story meant. As far as she could tell, it meant nothing. And to proceed as though it were otherwise, to make her catastrophe mean, would have been to inflate it, to turn it into something it was not, to give it a power it had no right to possess. A power, although she didn't say this, over what was most human in her, that which defied her malfunctioning biology, its clockwork universe. But then I knew I had only an inkling of what she meant, of what it was like to see the world through one eye.

August withered to nothing, and my project with the jars also drew to a close. One Saturday morning I drove to the shores of a nearby pond, where I found a large mound of red ants frantically building or maintaining their home. There were a lot of small rocks around the periphery, and even though I remembered something about red ants being ferocious biters I told myself this was probably an urban myth. I picked up a half-dozen rocks and filled my penultimate jar with them. Goose shit was everywhere along the well-worn path to the water, and I startled a great blue heron as I made my way through the rushes. The same heron, wings spread wide, would glide in front of me when I returned to the car. I threw the jar as far as I was able into the middle of the pond, and the birds swam to the spot where the surface was spreading in thick rings. The jar sank, and the birds didn't pay me any more notice. By then a sunny rain was falling. It was pleasant, but I couldn't shake the feeling that I was out of place in it. That to nearly anyone who saw me at either pond, my behavior would be, if not utterly mystifying, just plain weird.

Back in the car with only one jar remaining, I drove a mile or so to a tall pagoda that rose above a nearby playground. For months I had been intrigued by the incongruous structure, plopped down in a working-class neighborhood, some hundred feet from Lefthand Creek. Armed with the last of the forty or so jars I disposed of that summer, I discovered a large brass plaque describing the five levels of compassion the structure symbolized: love, empathy, understanding, gratitude, and selflessness. At first glance, there seemed to be no good place to bury the jar, and a sign on one end indicated that I was not to enter the fenced area surrounding the pagoda, so I threw it onto the second level, empathy, where I thought a small ledge would catch it. Then, with the singular rattle of glass on metal, it began to roll down the roof. I hopped into the prohibited area, but not quickly enough. The jar broke into pieces on the cement before I could catch it. My immediate dilemma was to figure out what to do with the glass: should anyone have cut their foot on my poem, I wasn't sure, anti-poet or not, I could have forgiven myself. Less immediately, I was concerned that the pagoda of compassion had rejected my writing, but I also couldn't help thinking that the words of this particular poem had something to do with its fate. One line—*to loose my band of roaming wit*—may have wanted to teach me a lesson. Something about language and containment, perhaps. How a self needs a little interruption now and then, something approximately the opposite of burying a poem in a jar.

In fact I did hear from the sixth poet again, years after the feud had ended, when I had already been living in Pennsylvania for some time. I woke up early one morning suddenly inspired to write to her, to say I was sorry. What I was sorry for, and why I should apologize to the sixth poet of all people, wasn't clear to me. Maybe I was sorry that although I had spent thirty-five years on the planet at that point, I didn't know why I was alive. Or maybe I was sorry that I had lost touch with some vital part of myself, the part that had once tried, and failed, to be a poet, the part for whom language had been something of sixth sense, as it always is for poets, the real ones, anyway. She had worked, more than anyone, to teach me that practice of perception, but I had instead lapsed into the kinds of remarks made by second-rate minds, the sort for which Liu Xie had become famous. Maybe I felt that the squabble between the first and second poets had been a test of my mettle, and that rather than rise above it I had been as self-interested as everyone else, less a poet than a placeholder, more an apparatchik than an artist.

Who was I now, I wrote to the sixth poet, who had I once been? Which self or selves had I left behind? These had been active questions for me all along, at least since my time in the cabin, probably before. I had tried reclaiming the past and abandoning it, but I saw no easy way to join the present. Don't forget who you are, the sixth poet responded, breaking our silence in turn, unless you want to leave that self behind. I considered whether I did, whether I had once wanted to, whether it was even possible. In concluding her short note, in advance of the longer one she promised, she quoted the poet Charles Olson, his overheard epigraph to *The Maximus Poems*: *All my life I've heard / one makes many*. But many, she wrote, also make one. Coming long after the events of that summer, but also premised upon them, and upon much else in my life up to that point, this was nothing short of a revelation.

## 6

The editor's invitation had come after the rejection, and even though the simultaneous push and pull in the man's emails stung him somewhat, he was soon standing on the platform waiting for the train at the Lancaster station. A year had passed but he still hadn't fully projected himself into this future, found himself, as usual, clinging to the past. By what design had he moved, that summer of 2012, to the city of his grandmother's birth, the site of his grandparents' courtship? His mother remembered its little rowhouses and the daily walk she took, when visiting, to the market, where her grandfather bought the day's provisions. It's always been a working-class town, she told him, but what, he wondered, were his grandfather's impressions of it when, after leaving the navy in February of 1945, he arrived to attend the college where his grandson now found himself teaching?

He thought the platform probably looked unchanged, minus the elevators, as though if one ignored the surroundings, and the fact that train travel itself had become something of an anachronism, it could be almost any moment during the past century. He settled, quite by accident, into the quiet car at the front of the train, watching as they rolled out of the city he still thought of as his grandmother's, not his own. Cities always looked dirtier by train, he thought, passing a large open lot lined with the sort of enormous steel girders you see below bridges, whereas the countryside always looked, albeit deceptively, cleaner. And almost on cue they were moving through undulating fields full of working Amish families, fathers and sons steering their horse-drawn plows, mothers and daughters hanging the wash out to dry.

That morning he was listening to Erik Satie as he waited, as he rode, even as he watched several times in quick succession, courtesy of Amtrak's internet, a YouTube clip of the closing scene of *Rocky*. It was like a disturbance for him, this music, an agitation he found himself clinging to and simultaneously struggling to shake. Its mood saturated even the film's sense of triumph, to the point that there was something vaguely depressing about Stallone charging up the steps at the Philadelphia Museum of Art, where the editor had suggested meeting that afternoon. I'll be nondescript, he wrote, but you can find me at the large bronze Amazon along the right side. She's fighting off a panther, he said. I'll be at her feet.

The train, or at least his car, was full of well-dressed people he took for commuters. Everyone had a laptop open or a tablet on. Most, like him, were wearing headphones. The two men behind him spoke nearly in whispers, having already been scolded for talking by a round, white-haired woman a few rows up. Soft as the music was, he could hear the outlines of their talk, the cadences, but not much else. He rode in something of a daze and so couldn't tell at what point the scenery outside his window shifted from farmland to suburb, but once the change came it was all he could see, how one mode had given way to another, was giving way, maybe, even then.

In his initial email the editor had offered extended feedback, a generous gesture that initially struck him as a bit too magnanimous, although this was undoubtedly a product of being told what he didn't want to hear. Don't get me wrong, the editor said, I admire the work, and what I have to say doesn't contradict but rather extends from that admiration. And then he proceeded to outline, with cutting precision, the three areas he felt were lacking. The first of these he called *Style*. The prose, as you must know, the editor wrote, is extraordinarily well wrought, but the Sebaldian harp is a heavy one to strum. The line stunned him, and coming as it did at the top of the email it shaped his reaction to the rest. He hadn't been able to set the criticism aside, moreover, and in the month after receiving the note the thought that he had been parroting an early idol gave him pause, so much so that he hadn't since made any progress. He slowly saw the other implications. He had been anxious about the influence of his father and grandfather, that one of their forms of restraint would become his own, but he still wanted to break through it, whatever that meant, wanted, in his life and his writing, to trace a new itinerary, mark out a new path.

Besides, he thought, looking around him on the train, Satie's ghostly music reverberating in his ears, Sebald would never have written this book. It was too personal, for one thing. Sebald kept his readers at a cautious distance, inviting and defying them to identify the narrators of his work with his person, when they were not the same; if one wanted to know the man, one had to step back from the text and see the patterns his mind, like tracks across a snowy field, had left on the work. Perhaps he had learned his lessons too well, but then had he been Sebald he would have looked at the passengers on the train, businessmen bent over their devices, and drawn some connection, however tentative, between the information that had become almost atmospheric and the virtual seclusion, even as they shared the same air, of one passenger from another. Though of course there he was, thinking that thought, in the third person to boot.

The editor's second criticism had been more thematic in nature. This he called *Focus*. These are familiar themes, he wrote, familiar fathers. Herzog pulls a steamship over a mountain. Thoreau retreats to his cabin. And in some dim suburban basement a father, a father's father, extinguishes himself. Had the editor missed, he wondered, the early nod to Kara Walker's silhouettes, to the plastic hut in the Colorado mountains, a far cry from Thoreau's handmade one in Walden? This all started with the gap between the real and the simulated, he wanted to say, but remembering himself, a true Midwesterner, he kept quiet. There is the expectation of connection, he thought as the train rolled through the wealthy mainline suburbs, of authenticity, of relation, but there is instead this substitution and simulation, the degraded, distorted approximations with which one makes do. Something unbridgeable lies between us, and the very bonds of our neighborliness contain the seeds of our estrangement. We're often left without much of a foothold in each other. On some level we simply refuse to be known.

As the train pulled into the 30th Street Station, he wondered what Sebald would have made of the structure, its atmosphere of Depression-era public works project, how he would have connected it, if at all, to the industrious workers on the train. He put away his headphones and rode the escalator up into the mammoth waiting room, where he felt caught again in a recursion of time. Only by now he was less in the loop of his father's family than his mother's, and though there was no particular reason why the place should have occasioned this realization, as he fumbled first toward one exit then another, eventually walking out onto Kennedy Boulevard, which dead-ends at the station, he felt he had long before made some error in judgment that he was only now, 1,800 miles from where he began, coming to recognize. The editor had maybe been right about the fathers but for the wrong reason: how had he missed all the mothers, the women whose lives had shaped his own, melding with it, mutating it, endowing it with substance? How had he missed his mother's father, for that matter, the only grandfather he had ever known?

As he stood on one in a row of bridges over the Schuylkill River, trying to get his bearings in the unfamiliar city, he considered what he knew. Names and dates, mostly. A first place medal in the 800-yard dash. His birthday (January 15, 1921), as well as his wife's (October 31, 1924). The GI Bill. Brainerd, Duluth, and St. Paul, Minnesota. Lancaster, Pennsylvania. Nyack, New York. Armstrong Cork Company, the employer of Harry Wolfe, his grandmother's father (full name: Harry Napoleon Bonaparte Wolfe), then his grandmother's employer during World War II. It all began, according to the corporate history he pulled up on his smartphone, in a tiny two-man cork-cutting shop in Pittsburgh, but although its founder, Thomas Armstrong, was a pioneer in brand names—stamping Armstrong on each cork as early as 1864—the Lancaster site where his grandmother and great-grandfather worked was, as he read on the bridge, a linoleum plant.

He knew that his grandparents had moved from Lancaster to Nyack, where his aunt and uncle were born in 1948. His grandfather trained to be a missionary, but then something happened and he no longer wanted to be a missionary. The story he remembered was that his grandfather couldn't learn another language, but his guess, as he descended a stairwell to the Schuylkill, was that one of them got spooked. They had young twins, after all, and he remembered how difficult it had been for his grandmother to live in Egypt in the '80s, when his grandfather was working with the Coptic Christians. In 1950, they moved to St. Paul, Minnesota, and his grandfather became a seminarian. After his ordination, they lived in the smallest of towns—Blomkest, Minnesota (his mother was born in nearby Wilmur), and Kiron, Iowa—before settling in Chicago in the early 1960s. There was never much money. They had been children of the Depression, and in working-class families like his, those years, followed by the war, left certain indelible prints. They may have learned to be suspicious of good news. They had undoubtedly learned to make do.

At the bottom of the steps, he joined the trail along the river. The path was jammed with joggers and office workers, and he marveled at the transformation of what had been industrial wasteland into yuppie playground. Here, capitalism had reclaimed what it had driven into ruin, and it seemed entirely consistent with this trend that other areas of the city he had seen from the train had not at all been reclaimed but appeared rather to have been driven further into dereliction. And as though to prove to him something he had already intuited, he saw an old man lying on the ground, attended by a couple of young paramedics. The man had the look of someone who hadn't looked well in a long time, not unlike his grandfather, perhaps, waiting out his death in the tiny room with the tacky valance over the window. He wished, walking past the bent bodies of the paramedics, there was something he could do, either for the old man or his grandfather, but all I can do now, he thought, is to put one foot in front of the other.


The way his mother told it his grandmother was a gifted musician who played piano in the churches where his grandfather ministered. She practiced at home, and one day his grandfather, writing his sermon for the week, heard the sound of the piano coming from the other room. He imagined his grandfather tried to tune it out at first, but eventually it clouded his mind to the point where he could no longer think from the table to the pulpit. He stood up, walked over to his grandmother, and asked if she would please cut out the racket. She more than obliged. She never touched a piano again. But he also remembered the gentle, intuitive woman she became, or reprised, in her later years. His grandmother's mother, born in nearby Lititz, had been a proto-feminist, writing poetry and working with the poor, and her father, also born nearby, in Columbia, Pennsylvania, had taken care of their daughter and the house that still stands at 142 East James Street.

After her sudden collapse from a stroke in 2003, whatever happiness his grandfather had known, and he suspected it had been relatively little, evaporated. It was as though he slowly but progressively lost interest in living. She had kept him in check, his tendencies toward stubbornness and self-absorption—was it this he missed most, even if he missed it unconsciously? His grandfather had immediately stopped wearing his hearing aids after she died, slowly descending into the deepest kind of silence, in the wake of which the family could only speculate about those things he had never spoken of, and now never would. It was possible, for example, that his mother, Olga, got pregnant from one of her half-brothers, but she was also working at the time as a live-in housekeeper for a man in Brainerd named Cohn. If this man Cohn was his great-grandfather, he thought, now following the fork in the trail that led to the museum, why suppress Cohn's name on his grandfather's birth certificate and invent, instead, a last name, Lawrence, that had no connection to anyone in the town? The fact that Cohn was Jewish, or more simply that he had gotten his housekeeper pregnant? Then again, there could be a mystery man hovering just beyond the threshold of history, lost forever behind that open door. Olga did have two other children with two other men, so who's to say.

He remembered then, as the *Rocky* steps came into view, the letter in his mother's lock box, addressed to his uncle, to be opened only after his grandfather had died. For years, he couldn't help but wonder whether he had known who his father was all along, and whether this letter, inserted in the longstanding gap between him and his son, admitted it. Whatever the letter said, he felt the weight of a secret kept hidden for nearly a century only added to the sadness of the man's old age, the sadness that his father's father had avoided. The slow diminution of his grandfather's presence in the world had been a humiliating process, and he wore the marks of its indignity plainly. His clothes were stained with it, and his smile—he had had several rotten teeth removed—was riddled with it. The last meal they had eaten together was a wordless affair on his grandfather's part, but how could he blame him? The man's pique at having been detained here so long and in such demeaning conditions gave his silence both its tragedy and its power. Climbing upward now, toward the museum, he thought that his living grandfather would be no less mysterious in the end than the one who, twenty-five years earlier, had chosen to end his life rather than face the disgrace it had, in his own eyes, become. That his other grandfather had never admitted to knowing the identity of his own father was only the most obvious of ways in which, even after his death, he would perplex those who loved him. The deeper, more ingrained mysteries would be no less acute for his absence.

What does it mean to be a father, to have a father, to lose a father, to have your father withheld from you? The living try to fill these holes or maybe just trace their outlines. But in doing so a self doubles, and redoubles: I find at my inception the selves of my parents, he thought, and then, further back, those of theirs. And so on and so on, and so the past, too, is peopled by doubles, made up of dead-ends.


In truth, he had forgotten about *Rocky* before reading the editor's email, but now, looking down the expanse of the Benjamin Franklin Parkway, he saw the film's setting in the birthplace of American democracy as a deliberate bit of symbolism: how, in the land of liberty, to liberate oneself from the ranks? He had thought to take advantage of the chance to visit the museum and so arrived early that morning, long before his scheduled meeting with the editor. He was surprised to see, at the top of the stairs, a young couple pantomiming Stallone's gestures for their digital cameras. There were a few minutes before the museum opened, and as he sat taking in the Parkway, which led from the museum steps to the ornate city hall—complete with a twenty-seven-ton statue of William Penn on top—he considered what it said about the place that its periphery was overtaken by *Rocky* reenactments, but that its wings and galleries were likely all named after wealthy patrons.

This initial misgiving, once inside, colored nearly everything he saw. The many rooms and hallways seemed to discourage delight, and the building almost had the feeling of a courthouse, which was in perfect keeping with his impression, while climbing its central staircase, that he was about to be judged. Museums, he thought, with their pretensions of culture, wretched architecture, and repellent politics, must be at times the worst places on Earth to see art, particularly if one should be so unfortunate—as he was that morning— to visit on the day of a special exhibition, during which it becomes impossible, due to the crowds shuffling through the galleries with their strapped-on headsets, to actually see any of the work on the walls. We hang paintings, he remembered from Georges Perec, to defuse walls, to make them disappear, but inevitably the paintings become part of the walls and their power as pores evaporates. As he walked, first through one wing then the other, he imagined a museum in which the paintings, or some portion of them, were rotated every fifteen minutes. A museum where the works were organized not by period, but alphabetically by last name. A museum built mostly or entirely of glass. A museum without windows or doors. He even imagined, and this was his favorite, a museum of possible museums.

That month there was an exhibition of Gauguin, Cézanne, and Matisse. His ticket was for 11:30, and as he stood waiting in line to get in, he worried that the bird the building most resembled, with its outstretched wings, was a vulture. An open-air museum would be infinitely more pleasant, he thought. Either that or find a way to bring the streets in. One employee, a dapper man in his twenties, told him that the line was long because everyone had had the same thought about beating the crowd, but that in trying to beat the crowd they had created it. In the end, he spent more time waiting for the exhibition than looking at it. The place was so tightly packed he fled, quickly walking back to the bright, airy corner of the museum where he had earlier found a cycle of ten paintings by Cy Twombly channeling the whole Homeric cast. For maybe twenty minutes he sat in front of a big red fireball of anger, which possessed the richness and texture of a pool of blood, and underneath which was written: *The fire that consumes all those before it.* If it isn't the same rage as that which leads young men, with increasing regularity, to gun down some dozen of their compatriots, no matter. The blood is still red, and it flows no less freely today than it did three thousand years ago. Is this a piece of a previous life, he wondered, or a life yet to come?

Out on the front steps once more, somewhat disgusted by the whole experience, he now saw several groups reenacting the *Rocky* scene. Some well-built men appeared to be training for real battles of some sort, if not boxing matches then those cage fights in which men peck at each other like roosters until one is nearly dead. They sweated and grunted up and down the steps in a series of exercises that made remarkable use of the rather plain device of the stair.

Sitting there at the base of the Amazon, wearing a white t-shirt and an open pink button-down, was the editor, a thin man whose face and head bore a uniform layer of stubble. They shook hands and began walking slowly down the parkway. They almost immediately fell to talking, as they strolled, about an interview the editor had just been listening to with the poet Marie Howe. She recounted seeing her brother John dying of AIDS—blind in one eye, unable to walk, and weighing all of 90 pounds. He had heard the same interview the previous fall, he told the editor, when he was commuting back and forth to his teaching job in Denver. He remembered tearing up, he said, as he parked the car on a side street near his office. Howe had just recounted a moment when her brother, lying in the hospital bed, looked up at her and said, *This is not a tragedy, Marie. I'm a happy man.*

The editor admitted he had also choked up a bit from the emotion in her voice and the idea, beautiful in every way, that one can suffer without suffering, that some places within us don't tarnish. But, the editor asked, is it true? I place myself in John's shoes: would I be able to say, as he did, that pain is inevitable but suffering a choice? He wondered if John himself believed it, or whether he wasn't putting on a brave face for his sister. The circumstantial measures, anyway—wealth and health among them—didn't apply in John's case, and while he may have been genetically predisposed for joie de vivre, it would also seem that John's happiness was a feat of psychological strength. They were passing the Barnes Foundation's new museum just then, and the editor stopped to explain the controversy surrounding it. Some said it had been a coup by the city's cultural elite, who had conspired to steal the collection from the foundation that administered it, but to the editor it seemed that, as usual, nearly everyone involved had missed the point. The art didn't give a damn. That's what made it art.

But the idea that happy people don't experience tragedy, the editor said, picking back up the thread of their conversation, or don't experience it *as* tragedy, is plainly wrong, and in refusing to call his death tragic, you could argue John points to the fact that it is, even if he doesn't see it as such. For him, John's apophatic gesture—*let's not speak of the tragedy*—was an object lesson in the complexity that makes up real happiness. In Howe's version of the story, he went on, the causal term appears to have been omitted: *This is not a tragedy* because *I am a happy man*. But in his mind the missing term was a conjunctive one: *This is a tragedy* but *I am a happy man*. Such is the nature of happiness, the editor concluded, fleeing out the back door as soon as it's arrived.

The final and most damning criticism the editor had offered in his initial email, before suggesting that it would be better to discuss it in person, over coffee or a walk or both, which we could certainly do if you're ever in Philly, the editor had said, was the failure to resolve and reorient the conflicts throughout. He called this *Form*, and went on to write that he noticed an almost willful refusal of the narrative arc the reader had intuited from the first page: he saw it, correctly, as a crisis of feeling, inherited from his fathers, instilled by his education, enacted in his writing, but shattered by his son. You wallow in yourself a little and that gets ponderous and old, he had written. Maybe you need to find a way out by the book's end, a way to dramatize or enact that escape, to set us all in motion—to say, look, this is intractable, it's wide-ranging, there's no escape, and yet see me escaping it, even as it continues to shape everything, especially the escape.

It was only after sitting for some time at the outdoor café on Logan Square, however, looking back toward the museum they had just left, that the subject of the manuscript came up. Nearby, a small boy wearing a Spider-Man t-shirt, maybe three years old, was throwing a fit at the fountains that spouted up from the pavement. His father was trying to calm him down, but his efforts at squelching the tantrum were failing horribly, and he seemed to be losing his own temper. He sympathized, he told the editor, having been there many times. And so, the editor asked, taking another sip from his iced coffee, when your son grows emotional, when he lashes out like that, how do you handle it? The question cut to the core of the problem, he said, the one he had spent years dancing around in his prose. In exactly the wrong way, he finally answered. He got angry about his anger, annoyed by his tears. You don't write about this explicitly in the book, though, the editor said. Maybe you should. But how, he asked, getting back to the real dilemma, do I escape an arc that continues beyond the confines of the writing, which is only an extension of that arc to begin with? Instead of answering the question, the editor watched the children who were squealing with delight as first one fountain gushed forth then another. He took a long drag on his straw then proposed writing a scene in which he, too, the editor, became a character in the book, a scene in which the editor's exhortations served as signposts toward or escape hatches from the discursive traps throughout. He might make a good character, the editor suggested, and their impromptu afternoon, carefully handled, could certainly make for a memorable episode—inserted as a matter of counterpoint, say, or maybe filigree.

Before long they were wending their way back toward the station, through Rittenhouse Square and the quiet cobbled streets just south and west of it, eventually reaching the walkway along the Schuylkill River, which they then followed back to the station, pausing briefly on a bench across from the city's former central post office, now a branch of the IRS, the editor told him. It made for a lovely composition, they agreed, the river moving slowly south, the lines of highway traffic coursing both ways beneath the building, and the large gathering of gulls coming and going from its roof—so many modes of movement within the same frame.

It was nearly time to catch their trains, but neither man moved. How many thousands of gallons of water flowed past as they sat there, how many hundreds of cars? It was modern life itself, the editor supposed, that turned a person into a walking paradox, at once forward-looking and caught in a past with no prospect of progress. The conversation was returning, in a way, to the dilemma they'd discussed in the square. Whatever the self is, the editor said then, still looking out at the river, wherever it lives, and however it comes into being, one wonders if, left to its own devices, it doesn't inevitably turn inward— if, without some counterbalancing gravity, it doesn't become a kind of black hole, drawing everything into it.

He then remembered, as though the editor's words had unsettled something in him, an image from his morning at the museum, a modest white outline of a woman set against a brown background. She had two faces, he said, two necks descending from them. One appeared to be a projection from the other, a stenciled cutout, or a mask. Maybe, he said, the two of them standing in silent accord, each of these—projection, cutout, and mask—is real, and the active, visible self is always a variable version of a hidden one. Unless this is a distortion as well, the editor added, in which case where is the self if it is always only the projection and amplification of certain of its parts? They were walking now, ascending the ramp to Market Street. Like the negative from whose inversions of light a positive image can be produced, the editor concluded, maybe the self must be enlarged and reversed, through contact with others.


Back at the station, having parted ways at the entrance to the local SEPTA trains, he sat on one of the long wooden benches, not unlike church pews, in the atrium. He thought about how earlier that day he had felt, emerging into the room on the escalator, caught in a recursion of time, and he remembered how some elephants return, year after year, to the site of a matriarch's death, that in their grief they stir up her bones. He had been moved, a few days earlier, by an account of how an older elephant's death creates ripples in younger generations, how in South Africa there have even been instances, previously unobserved, of orphaned young bulls goring rhinos then mounting them. Every ten minutes or so, another train would leave, and the big board announcing departures would shuffle loudly through the letters. People began lining up near the escalator leading down to his train, even though there were still twenty minutes before it left. The line slowly grew longer, and after a few minutes he joined it. When he eventually settled into the front car, which was no longer the quiet one, he saw how what the museum employee had said earlier about the crowd applied to the many empty seats on the train. And, in a different way, to the elephants.

He began again to listen to Satie, trying to recapture a bit of that morning's peaceful daze, but there were rowdy kids at the back of the car and, just in front of him, a gaggle of middle-aged women returning from a day of shopping, their purchases stowed in the bins above them. He soon had to give up on the music, which couldn't overcome the ruckus, but was it not also the case, he wondered, that he had to give up on his temperament? Perhaps this was part of the arc the editor had been talking about, the resolution he wanted to see, in which the moody, insulated self he had both inherited and cultivated was cast aside or consumed, like a chrysalis. Just then a towheaded boy of five or six ran down the aisle making shooting motions with his hands, and when the boy pointed a finger at him—*pew, pew*—he tilted his head sideways, closed his eyes, stuck out his tongue. The boy giggled and went on his way.

It was all he could do, when he finally returned to Lancaster that day, to keep putting one foot in front of the other. These are the streets, he thought, rutted or not, I live on. The streets my mother walked as a girl (and her mother before her, and her mother before her) are the same ones my son is walking now. I am crossing, as a teacher, the same hallways my grandfather crossed as a student. He didn't know what to make of the coincidence of his life there, but his emergence from the station into the August sun seemed to portend a shift within him from the dead to the living, the past to the present, from the dark entities of his family's history into the light of a new generation.

Maybe it's enough to say, he thought, remembering that view of the river, what the editor had said there, that no one is quite what we imagine them to be, nor are they what they imagine themselves to be. Or rather, that they, and we, are all of these imaginings plus something else, something that doesn't shake in any storm. To know this is more than a matter of selves hidden and seen, of histories opened and closed. To know this, somehow, is forgiveness.

## 7

That December I had been rereading *Walden*, while visiting my in-laws in Florida, when I got a call from a man who said his name was Kevin, and that he was Naomi's husband. I fell into a beach chair next to my wife, gripping the phone tightly. We had driven out to Sanibel Island, and in fact I had been reading aloud a memorable passage punctuated by Thoreau's exhortation not to loiter in winter when it's already spring. That morning it had been raining on and off, and our son had gone for a walk with his grandparents to the old lighthouse and fishing pier down the beach. The service would take place that week in Boston, where Naomi had grown up. She would have wanted me to come, Kevin said before hanging up, and although my wife didn't quite understand it—we had only met once, she protested—I insisted on making the trip. That night, as I lay in bed, unable to sleep, I realized the drive would bring me quite near to Walden.

On the day of the funeral, I took a long walk across the Common, through the public garden, and up the mall on Commonwealth Avenue, before cutting back on Newbury Street. I lingered a bit too long over a coffee near Copley Square, and when I returned to my car on the far side of the Common, I saw a parking cop putting a ticket on my windshield. It was too late, he said, the ticket had printed. I was just leaving, I objected. So go, he said, walking away. It was a scene I saw repeated that afternoon in Concord, where, after my trip to the pond, I was struck by the number of police on the street, many of them handing out tickets. There had been two funerals in Concord that day, as I learned in a little place called Helen's, and the town was packed to the gills. On any other day, the waitress said, I would have had almost no trouble finding a spot.

In walking through the Back Bay that morning, I had thought to work off my dread prior to the funeral, but the ticket—and this was the sort of thing I had been doing for years—threatened to encase me in it. I could see how I had often been simultaneously too isolated and too sensitive for my own good, touchy even, and it was partly my suspicion that my son had inherited a similar temperament that had begun to inspire me, as much as possible, to maintain an even keel. But I was still learning the tricks of equilibrium, and it wasn't easy, for instance, to shake the hands of Naomi's husband and daughters, her parents and in-laws, most of whom had no idea who I was or what I was doing there. Kevin was warm—he even said he was grateful—but this only managed to make me more uncomfortable, as though his kindness was a considered response to my tenuous position. He introduced me to Naomi's mother as her pen pal, and then the three of us stood in confusion before I explained that I had met her daughter a few years earlier, at a point when I was feeling nearly as desperate as she was. This only muddled matters further. I said that I had seen her making a sketch in the National Gallery, that we had struck up a conversation, even had lunch together, and that we had occasionally exchanged emails ever since, at which point Kevin told me, even though I didn't see how it could possibly be true, how much my friendship had meant to her. Her mother, who must have been about sixty, with smooth, almond skin, wrapped her arms around me. I know, she kept saying, I know, but what she knew escaped me.

Outside the old stone church, I realized I had not made the trip to mourn my friend exactly, since it was hardly my place to mourn her. Instead, I had come to pay homage both to her and to the person I had been when we met. On the surface, I was there to participate in a ritual farewell, which, watching her young daughters shake the hands of strangers, would clearly be different from the actual, protracted one. It was a shameful consequence of our lives, I thought, that they had been drained of ceremony, or rather that our ceremonies continued but had been drained of their power to move us. The service, in its pomp and vanity, left me cold. How endlessly we reinvent ourselves, as though each day were this day only, and not part of a pattern. It would seem today can teach us nothing about tomorrow, nor yesterday about today. What Naomi's death required of me would not be the same as what future deaths might—my grandfather's, for instance, which would finally come a few months later, in early April. Her death could tell me nothing I didn't already know, and yet I felt the responsibility to honor it, and her, as though some mysteries were more than intact and indeed were still sacred.

For days I had worried about the trip to Concord. What good could it possibly do in my present state of mind to visit the house where Emerson penned the line about envy being ignorance and imitation suicide. Unless the expedition was merely to get me away from my desk, but for that there were parks nearby and a child who demanded, as children will, almost constant attention. In my more rational moments I knew that I had hatched another in a series of escape plans and then, as always, justified my prolonged flight on the flimsiest of grounds. In this instance, my excuse for leaving the real and figurative dishes in the sink just a bit longer—that I would be plumbing the depths of literary history—was flagrant enough that I had no trouble seeing it as the evasion it was. I may have known in the abstract that a person can't avoid his life, at least not for long, but over the years this hadn't kept me from fabricating, consciously or not, various projects and ploys to take up my time, to keep me from meeting the daily demands of work and family.

Still, the trip came during what felt like a long sea change, if not in me then in my circumstances. Some tectonic shift was taking place, and more than understanding the mechanics of it I was merely trying to get my bearings. One phase of my life had all too clearly ended and another, less marked by contingency, appeared to be beginning. It seemed I was no longer who I had been, but also that that person had been a prophecy of myself as I was coming to be. In previous years I had maybe forgotten, as Thoreau warned me I might, that it is always the first person speaking. At least part of the change I felt consisted of the realization that there was probably nothing more ridiculous than to act, as they sometimes teach you in school, as though you had no self.

When I arrived at the pond, signs warned me alternately that the water was unguarded and that I could be fined for leaving the trail lining the shore. Other signs pointed the way to the site of the hut, not to be confused with the structure erected next to the parking lot. Both the signs and the replica seemed bizarre, but when I stopped at the gift shop to ask why the replica had not been built on the original site, everything was locked and one middle-aged man, upset at the closure, was angrily dialing a number on his phone. It's always like this, he told me, but it wasn't clear whether he meant the missing workers or something else. I walked down the hill, scanning the water through the trees, but it did not feel, as a friend had warned me it would, like just another pond. If you've seen one, you've seen them all, she'd said. As I stomped down the stone steps to the beach, it was as though some unexplored ocean opened in me. Whatever transformation I had undergone or was undergoing seemed to express itself here, or else the change reflected back at me from the surface of the pond.

And yet something jarred me. While it made a certain logistical sense to have all the buildings in one place, the artificiality of the replica, and its displacement, was both in line and at odds with the posted insistence that everything at Walden Pond be kept close to its original state. Clearly, this wasn't the case. For one thing, the pond had not yet frozen entirely over, as Thoreau said it had much earlier in the season, a century and a half prior. It was cold, but not frigid, and the sun occasionally peeked out from the high, wispy clouds that did not so much obscure the blue as veil it. I couldn't tell whether the ice was freezing or thawing, but it made a sound that reminded me of the songs of humpback whales, and it was no less true in this case that I—along with the rest of the world, perhaps—was unable to decipher what it meant. Though Thoreau recorded hearing the same eerie whooping in the ice as it shifted, the men he described as coming by train to gather it for the city summer would have had a meager harvest were they to have come that year. The pond was clear enough that I met two men fishing in open water on the far side, wrappers from Dunkin Donuts straws on the path above them. The trains that run on the west side of the pond—which had, in earlier incarnations, both bothered and delighted Thoreau—passed along the rails twice in the hour I spent on the path. A boat ramp had been constructed on the east side of the pond, and there was also a seasonal bathhouse near Walden Street, which divided the parking lots and the replica of the cabin from the pond itself. Standing on the beach below the road, I could hear large trucks passing by, delivering lumber or hauling broken-down cars. The pond was still lovely, but there were abominations like an automated parking machine and everywhere I turned I encountered a fence.

By the 1840s, writes E.O. Wilson, a resident of nearby Lexington, Walden Woods was already a sliver of its former self, hemmed in on all sides by former forests cleared for fuel and farmland. In Thoreau's time the trees around Walden, he says, were scraggly second-growth descendants of the giants that had lined the pond until the middle of the eighteenth century. While the wolf and wolverine may have disappeared from Massachusetts, Wilson is heartened by the relative health of the microcosm: ants, spiders, centipedes, worms, mites, fungi, and, at a more minute level, billions of bacteria in a thimbleful of sand. These strata of the living world have changed very little in a thousand years, Wilson writes, but this may be cold comfort, considering that, in sum, the living world is dying. If our lives, he continues, have always been an insoluble problem, a dynamic process in search of an indefinable goal—if they are neither a celebration nor a spectacle but rather, as George Santayana wrote, a predicament—then one ought to add, as a footnote to the list of nearly two thousand species found by Wilson and others one recent July, our amorphous teleology as an element of the landscape that remains unchanged.

The course of human history may have amplified matters, but the predicament we face is the one that led Thoreau to Walden in the first place, his sense that a person's life is the answering of a question he can't quite make out, and that, more often than not, society foreshortens the answers. He saw little in the improvements of modernity to get excited about, as they had not managed, he believed, to alter the basic facts of existence. For him, our inventions were improved means to unimproved ends, but they also produced, as a side effect, an epidemic of anxiety. We do not ride on the railroad, as he put it, it rides on us. It may have been that he spotted the symptoms in himself and so went to Walden to take the cure.

In one famous passage, he wrote that he went to the woods to live deliberately, to front only the essential facts of life, and to see if he could learn what it had to teach, and not, when he came to die, discover that he had not lived. I did not wish to live what was not life, he wrote, living is so dear. It was never his plan, however, to enact a permanent escape. His retreat to the woods was the distancing effect necessary to seeing things as they were and not as he, or others, would prefer them to be. Only by estranging himself from his life could he face those facts and, hopefully, use them as a guide when he became a sojourner in civilized life once more. But there was a deeper dimension to this estrangement, embodied in what Wilson insists was never a pond but a lake. Thoreau noted that its depth is remarkable for so small an area, yet not an inch of it could be spared by the imagination. The question is whether, as the deep and pure symbol he believed it to be, it fathomed the unfathomable or merely conceived of it, since given the least license, the mind dives deeper and soars higher than nature goes. Thoreau knew the breadth and depth of the pond, and it was no deeper or wider than the dimensions he fastidiously recorded. And yet, didn't he, in writing *Walden*, make it both wider and deeper?

At the same time that we are earnest to explore and learn all things, we require that all things be mysterious and unexplorable, that land and sea be infinitely wild, unsurveyed and unfathomed by us because unfathomable—even as we proceed to survey and to fathom them. The human predicament is largely a matter of seeing ourselves through our imponderables, as though from outside, creating a vantage from which to outline our edges. It is necessary that certain pools should be larger than what contains them, and that from within these bodies, or their reflections, the human world should appear smaller, and stranger, than it otherwise does. We need to witness our own limits transgressed, Thoreau believed, and to see some life pasturing freely where we never wander.

I was reminded, as I walked, of the pilgrimage to Mount Kailash, in western Tibet, made annually by many Buddhists, Hindus, and others, who believe that circumambulating the mountain will bring them good fortune. Months earlier, I had seen footage of the pilgrims in a Werner Herzog film, *Wheel of Time*, but in the flurry of images with which I had since been bombarded, I had forgotten all about them. As I passed an older couple navigating an icy patch of the trail, copies of *Walden* in hand, images of those who make the thirty-mile trek around the mountain while performing body-length prostrations came immediately to mind, less for their similarity to my own mini-pilgrimage than for the utter disparity between my obeisance and their own. I was not about to lay myself flat in the snow and mud at Walden, but the necessity of completing the circuit, of making the whole trip around the pond, in spite of the pressure I felt to get home, overtook me, not least because of the somber atmosphere from which I had only just emerged and to which, without knowing it, I was about to return.

But why, I asked myself as I approached the site of the original hut, am I in a rush to get home, and how much of my life has consisted of such hurrying? I sat down on one of a number of large rocks that led down from the path to the pond and tried, for the second time that day, to right myself in stormy waters. What had Naomi meant to me, and what did I owe her now? I thought again of her daughters, and was suddenly thankful for my own parents, their endurance. I felt also, from across the hundreds of miles that separated us, both the responsibility I had to my son and the precarious bundling of blood and bone and breath that made it all possible. I remembered, there on the rock, that the edition of *Walden* I had at home was not the newer, well-designed one I had with me, but the book whose cramped text I had first read some ten years earlier when I borrowed it from my father one winter and never returned it. I could see how I had been a fool, maybe even how, in writing the pages already taking shape in my mind at Walden, I would continue to be one, but I also felt there was no alternative to muddling along, clinging here and there to the scraps of what I had, however briefly, been privileged to grasp. How many could say they had been allowed even that? The wind whistled a little in the trees. A dry leaf rattled across the thin ice in front of me. Then it was as though I heard distant church bells ringing, slow and solemn, calling me to attention. I took stock of the path in front of me. Everything would recur. I rose and kept walking.

Nine stone pillars, waist-high and linked together by a chain, marked the site. Someone had made a snow angel beside the enclosure, maybe the little girl darting about as her mother read the plaque describing the fate of the cabin, which was first moved to a nearby farm then dismantled for firewood. It also told of the discovery, in 1945, of the foundation for Thoreau's chimney, memorialized in the chained-off space with a kind of tombstone. As the sun cast shadows from the pillars to the north, across the empty space they demarcated, what had bothered me about the replica came into clearer focus: its prime virtue was to point at what was no longer there. The pillars, with their dinky little chain, did nearly the same thing, pointing across Walden Street to the structure that had been built, for convenience, next to the parking lot. It might have been better if they hadn't built the replica or made a show, albeit a modest one, of the hut's disappearance. But who among us could have abided it? How could we have kept ourselves from recreating the scene? Absences grow richer, one might argue, when we point to the places they hide, but at Walden I became aware, a bit late, of a part of me that felt some gaps in the record were better left in place. And although I knew this feeling would likely disappear as soon as I sat down at my desk at home, standing there in the sun and snow, I wrote in my little notebook that certain things were better left unsaid.

It was after leaving the cabin site that I encountered the two fishermen, who, when I asked if they had caught anything, told me it was nearly impossible not to. The pond was stocked with fish, they said, which I took to mean that none, or very few, lived in the water on their own anymore. Later, I read in a pamphlet distributed by the state that more than half a million people come to the pond each year, and that this has been the case since at least the 1930s. On the cover was a deceptively empty picture of the pond in summertime. That it showed none of the buildings, signs, or fences, combined with the slogan beneath—*It's your nature*—only confirmed my suspicions about the role human life now played on the planet. Whatever this pond was today, it had been shaped by the people who used it. Not nature, precisely, but *human* nature, writ large on the face of the Earth. Inevitably, I thought of my friend, and of the error that had occurred at a genetic level, which once set in motion only multiplied itself exponentially, until her body had been overtaken by a mistake. What could it mean to become the first people, the only people, to entirely disappear?

It would be easy for the fates to cut our threads, Thoreau wrote, with a little sharper blast from the north. His was a mind of winter, hemmed in by the necessity of creating the warmth to sustain it. Our own problem, to which I can only offer the most obvious solutions, is to tick the thermostat down a few notches, so that our kids don't boil in their skins. As molecules move more quickly when warmed, so the pace of our simmering lives has frenzied, but I couldn't say then, much less now, whether our degradation is a contributing cause or inevitable effect. Perhaps it is merely a symptom, as is the ruination of the natural world, of a still more insidious disorder, one that, unfortunately, will never be diagnosable from within, though its signs are written plainly without.


Rumination, my wife once told me, is a dangerous thing. She had heard a radio program about happiness recently, and among the least happy people were those whose thoughts circled back on themselves. Such people were also more likely to focus on negative experiences, which did not produce the desired effect of avoiding similar experiences in the future but seemed, conversely, to ensure their perpetuation. On the other hand, those who focused on positive experiences managed to have more of them, and so, in terms of one's happiness, the only time rumination did any good was when good things actually happened. If all that sounds like common sense, as it certainly did to me, consider my response to my wife, who had only spoken out of a concern for my mental health, which in recent years had been unpredictable. Rumination, I told her, is the only thing I'm any good at. She protested at the time, but—though I was thankful for the gesture—no more than necessary.

My thinking may be no less circular these days, but as it revolves I've taken to consoling myself with the thought that around every circle, as Emerson wrote, another can be drawn. In walking at Walden, I had drawn a circle around something larger than the pond, albeit a well-worn one, but in writing about it now I am drawing another circle around that circle, circumambulating the circumambulation. Our life is an apprenticeship to the truth, Emerson wrote, a self-evolving circle, which, from a ring imperceptibly small, rushes on all sides outwards to new and larger circles, without end. But there are other circles here, as at Walden, those that place me at the center, rather than the circumference. I'm not sure what to make of the space where these two, center and edge, overlap.

After I finished my rather late lunch at Helen's that day, I walked down the Cambridge Turnpike and stood in front of the boxy white structure Emerson called home for nearly fifty years. I am only an experimenter, he wrote in 1841, perhaps inspiring his younger friend who had recently moved home and transposed his name from David Henry. Do not set the least value on what I do, Emerson continued, or the least discredit on what I do not, as if I pretended to settle any thing as true or false. I unsettle all things. But as I stood there watching the handsome young caretaker move heavy black trash bags from one side of the yard to the other, I couldn't bring myself to walk through the gate. That was another story, another pilgrimage. Another circle I wasn't yet willing to draw around my life, or with it. I walked back to the center of town, wondering where my life would expand to from here, and found that my car had not, luckily, been ticketed.


However intense my experience, I am conscious of the presence and criticism of a part of me which, as it were, is not a part of me, but spectator, sharing no experience, but taking note of it, and that is no more I than it is you. When the play—it may be the tragedy of life—is over, the spectator goes his way. It was a kind of fiction, a work of the imagination only, so far as he was concerned. So wrote Thoreau in a journal entry from August 8, 1852, and as I drove away from Walden, I was possessed once more by this sense of being both inside and outside of my life, at once witness and participant, narrator and subject, fictive and real. And maybe it was this simultaneous presence and absence, this chasm running through the center of my life, that had made the crisis so protracted and difficult to handle. If only I could find the place where all my doubles met, but then *I* was that place, so maybe the contradiction wasn't a disorder of the self, a work of the imagination only, maybe it was the self: inside and outside, neighbor and stranger, part and whole.

As I rejoined the interstate near Lexington, I thought of that pair of photos of my father with his father. Few rites of manhood may be more cliché, but now Dad's words came back to me: their story was undoubtedly more profound as they lived it. I considered that while I never had any trouble printing out the first photo, I had a great deal with the second. Sometimes it wouldn't appear at all, as though the printer couldn't process the image, which was more or less what the error messages said on the pages that often printed in its place. Other times distortions emerged, pixelated beyond recognition. Because I had always taken my grandfather's smile as a hopeful emblem, I didn't know what to make of it when the picture wouldn't print.

The obvious explanation was that my parents sent it to me in an unreadable file format, but the less obvious one stemmed from the shape my grandfather had taken in my mind. I had tried to capture him not as he was but as I imagined him to be, to invent his depression so as to understand my own. That the happy photo wouldn't print, or would only print as digital static, suggested what I suspected all along: he would remain an unresolved figure for me, out of focus in those parts of him that could smile after catching a fish with my father. But there was another possibility. It may be that I didn't wanted to see my grandfather as a happy man, that I was incapable of imagining him as such. I had only found what I went looking for. Whatever else the photo's obstinacy meant, it did feel, there in the car, like an exhortation—delivered from beyond the grave—to widen the lens.

And then I remembered the children's book of which, for a short while, our son was particularly fond. It tells the story of Farmer Bailey, who accidentally hits what he thinks is a deer while driving home one fall day. When he stops the truck, he finds a man instead, but the stranger doesn't speak and when the doctor checks his temperature the mercury stays at the bottom. He has an uncanny knack with animals and children and while helping on the farm neither takes a rest nor breaks a sweat. Like my son, I was drawn to the picture, reproduced on the cover, of the stranger being served hot soup. Steam rises from the ladle and from the pot next to it. The stranger's eyes are wide open. For days after first getting the book from the library, I teased my son by opening my eyes very wide, like the picture. Each time he laughed and said, delighted, *the stranger opens his eyes*.

And then I'm piloting my rental car, a tiny silver Chevy, north along the interstate, past towns I once lived in, through the endless brown of the high plains in winter, a landscape drenched in sun, and all the while I am thinking, as though I can't figure out what the fuck I am doing here, *you can't go home again, you can't go home.* But then I'm not going home, I tell myself, I'm passing through. There's some mystery out here that remains unsolved, some business left unfinished. It's the first weekend in December 2014, and I've come to spend a night in the cabin where this book begins, then the next night in Walden. On the radio, Mick Jagger is singing that it's a drag, getting old, but I feel a little stoned, though I've only just gotten off the plane, so I hear him saying, incorrectly of course, that time is still on my side. Between the two vastly different worlds of these two otherwise similar songs, in the gap between the actual and the imagined, lies a route I know well.

At the exit for Highway 52, I get off the interstate and take the back roads, but it's only when I'm heading west that I realize I'm tracing a familiar itinerary, the route I took coming home from teaching in Denver. I used to count the fracking wells until I crossed the Boulder County line, where drilling dwindled, but I'm not paying much attention now. I'm too busy trying to figure out why I'm headed to the neighborhood where I lived when I drove these roads regularly. I thought I was done with the place, but now it's corkscrewing into me, or rather I'm seeing it's been stuck here all along.

Soon I'm back in the so-called New Urbanist community where we lived then, each street with a ridiculous name like 100 Year Party Court or Tenacity Drive, which is where we resided, fittingly enough, in a bright yellow and gray box of a building that arrived on the Front Range, as much of its architecture does, from sometime in the future. Exactly *whose* future still isn't clear to me, since the place was meant to mimic the neighborhoods of the past: safe, walkable streets with densely built houses and parks and playgrounds and businesses nearby, a place where you knew all your socially diverse neighbors and they knew you. In truth it was a bastion of white, upper-middle-class heterosexuals, essentially a subdivision called Prospect plopped down in the middle of what had until only recently been a cornfield. It was a little bubble of privilege in a town that was historically blue-collar, at least until nearby Boulder became untenable for just about everyone. You got more house for your money out here, people said, although money seemed to be the furthest thing from the minds of most of our neighbors, several of whom, good liberals though they were, came from serious money either back east or out west or abroad. Many were doctors or executives or called themselves entrepreneurs. One man we rather liked invented a device for sucking snot out of an infant's nose; his wife sold an invention of her own, a kind of sleeve you rolled onto your arms instead of using sunscreen.

For most of the nearly three years we lived there, my wife had the better job, which meant that between his first and third birthdays I was the one shuttling our son to the playground, struggling with mittens and boots, changing diapers and managing naps. We hadn't exactly planned for the arrangement but were nonetheless pleased with how twenty-first century we were, walking manifestations of our architecture. We saw so smugly the limitations gender roles imposed on those we knew: how women substituted their children's lives for their own, how their husbands surrendered the domestic field early in the morning to return only in time to put the kids to bed. Didn't these women have anything better to do, we wondered, than post pictures of their children online? Didn't these workaholic fathers understand the pressures they were putting on their wives? Our situation, we told ourselves, was more balanced, more rewarding. The only problem was that neither of us really liked it. When my wife railed against stay-at-home-moms—who can afford that, she would ask—her ire was blended with jealousy, and the sharpness I aimed at the men had something to do with the shame of not being one of them. Even in progressive Boulder women far outnumbered men at the playgrounds and it was a rare weekday when I was not the only man applying gobs of sunscreen to a kicking target.

It was around that time a recurring fantasy I'm not particularly proud of began to develop. Sometimes I imagine walking out on my life. My wife and my son. My job and my mortgage and my writing. I've imagined a life of menial jobs, maintaining my silence in a sunny place near the sea, or else wandering North America, a kind of walkabout in the vein of Mildred Norman, a.k.a. Peace Pilgrim, who spent roughly thirty years as a wandering ascetic. Or maybe the walkabout as I first encountered it at age seven or eight in the movie *Crocodile Dundee*, and much later, already a grown man, in the work of the writer Bruce Chatwin: the aboriginal rite of passage, typically undertaken by an adolescent male, equal parts ancestor worship, pilgrimage, and survival test. Of course at thirty-five I'm probably too old for most rites of passage, but then I underwent so few of them. I was too busy getting first one degree, then another, then another—unless you want to count those as rites, and I don't.

Leaving my family would be unforgivable, unconscionable, really, and at odds with the affection I feel for them. And yet the other day I was sitting in on a Toni Morrison seminar, taught by a colleague of mine; they were discussing *Beloved*, and the conversation turned to the reasons why Paul D leaves Sethe. The student presenters were facilitating discussion, but on this particular point my colleague, who's from Sierra Leone and whose speech has a natural gravitas (silence surrounds it), interjected. *Note the Morrisonian theme*, he said. *Men leave.* His inflections possess such an incantatory lilt that when he pronounced those two syllables I was suddenly under the spell of their logic, or perhaps I recognized that in my fantasy I have been.

In the animal world, a father that stays is a rarity, so perhaps it's a little unnatural, or counter to what maleness entails, to be a father or husband, which is less to excuse bad behavior than to commend the excellent fathers and husbands out there. On the other hand, one could argue that the bonds of monogamy arose out of the extraordinary demands of human children: the long gestation and protracted maturation practically require a second pair of hands. Love, in this light, may exist for the sake of the species: if husbands didn't love their wives and children, and vice versa, we may have died out long ago. This may be a cynical take, but it's my *fantasy* I'm talking about here and every fantasy operates under its own self-interested logic. The obvious suggestion is that I don't love my family and would willingly leave them, as I sometimes have, out of nowhere, in my dreams: *He walked out for cigarettes one day.* Only I don't smoke, I write.

Then again, perhaps the dream confirms not a lack of love but its presence: if only I didn't care about these people, I would be free (*you always say that you want to be free*) to pursue whatever glittering future on which my eyes came to rest. *Odi et amo*, Catullus famously wrote (*I hate and I love*), and the endurance of his observation speaks to the fact that although I may sometimes dream of departure, I never leave. Except that I do. In small ways. This trip, for example, 1,800 miles from home, or the daily one I take to the attic, before my wife and son are awake, squeezing in a few minutes of writing before the day begins. I *escape* into my work in ways my wife has more than once registered. The sheer amount of time it requires is immense, at least for me, and pursuing it has other effects as well: all those mornings when I'm sulky, those dinners when I'm absent, having given all I had to the page.

During those years we lived in Prospect, we spent a lot of time just walking around the neighborhood, usually after our son's afternoon nap. We had a few well-established routes that allowed for certain variations, but some landmarks featured in most walks. The planters outside the liquor store, for instance, or the block of mailboxes near the park. While he was interested in discovering new things, he also liked familiarity. When I took him to what would become our regular playground for the first time, he got grumpy pretty quickly, as though without any landmarks he couldn't navigate a way. He might have turned down a strange road, but only if he recognized the one we took to get there. His maps expanded little by little, but most days he was happy to walk to the parking lot on the eastern edge of the neighborhood, near the highway, where a large RV was parked for the better part of a year. One of the tires was flat, parts of the trim were peeling off, and rust was accruing in the wheel wells. Hanging from the back were mud-flaps that looked like hula skirts—our son would run his hands through them—and at his full height, he liked to put rocks and things in the hollow bumper. There was a sign in the window with a number to call *for any questions about this RV*, but there wasn't any indication it was for sale.

Sometimes he just walked around and around, pointing at it occasionally and saying *that, that*. To which I responded, *RV, RV*. It became such a fixture of our walks that he often made a beeline for it. I was fascinated by his fascination. It was as if he were learning the world by rote, returning again and again to the same objects, the same places, the same words. It was almost an obsession. Or an itch he simply had to scratch. When his little index finger reached out to touch it, I sometimes thought he was assuring the thing it was still there. Then some object would glimmer in the grass nearby and his attention would be diverted. Each time we walked away from it I couldn't help but note the faded name of the model printed near the front, which read, in big brown letters, *Encore*.

One day as we were heading home, an older man I'd never seen before and would never see again, came up to me and said, *You're blessed, you know*, then walked away, leaving me stunned on the sidewalk. At the time I didn't know that I agreed, or rather I didn't know how to bring myself to agree with what I knew was true. But now I'm back in this parking lot that also bored me immensely, a place I spent so much effort and imagination trying to flee. Maybe four years have passed since the RV disappeared, and I'm standing here taking in the new buildings that have gone up in the meantime. All at once I'm sitting first on one curb then another, sobbing in the parking lot. It occurs to me that, insomuch as I've wished away time, insomuch as I haven't felt as blessed as I've been, I have failed as a father. I can sit here wishing I could get those years back, I can resolve to be better, gentler, not so hard on my son, on myself, but I've been through this before, vowed to be more grateful, more open, exposing the space within, only to see it close down once more, as soon as life normalized and routine became rule again.

What if what I thought were the bad times were actually the best? I'm speaking aloud to the empty silver Chevy now, wiping the dampness from my cheeks.

I have lunch, against my wife's advice, in the Mexican place down the road from our old townhome. Something's happening here and I need to let it, I say, texting her from in front of the restaurant. The spot had once been a sushi joint, but after it went under the new owners had to do, surprisingly enough, little remodeling. My eyes are still red and damp, and first the hostess, then the waitress, offers me a tequila. I ask for a kale salad instead, served with goat cheese and spiced nuts and pears. I ask for a *gordita* stuffed with *rajas* and *crema*. But as I'm waiting the feeling from the parking lot returns: I'm too preoccupied with my own dilemmas to worry about those of others, too cerebral and self-involved to invest myself in the emotions of my wife or my son. I'm bad at loving them, at loving others. I'm much better at being a son, at taking my parents' love, which has always been boundless and absolute, the kind of love I'm best at receiving.

At the same time I suspect, starting in on my salad, that the screeching baby on the plane bothered me less than others. I had some compassion for the parents, who I knew would never see any of us again, and yet who no doubt felt, as I had when flying with a very young child, that they were the worst sort of imposition. I can understand the child's displeasure, even in its piercing urgency. Her necessity for expression and the total lack of words for it—these are things I can understand, even feel. But how much easier emotions are when they aren't your own, how much easier to have compassion when your failure as a parent or spouse, or what feels like it anyway, isn't on display. How much easier other people's children can be, other people's lives, how much easier one's own life would be if only one could see it from outside, as though in the pages of a novel, told perhaps in the third person. What I wouldn't give for a fuller glimpse of the arc I'm living, even if to see it would require that I divorce, or estrange, myself from it.

As I weigh into the *gordita*, I'm thinking about how when I first came to Colorado, in June of 2002, I wasn't yet twenty-three years old. My then-girlfriend and I had packed all our worldly belongings, which didn't amount to much, into our red Subaru. We got married the following year, the second and last of the MFA program I came to Boulder to complete. It was a magic time, full of ferment and possibility, but when we left in the summer of 2004 the spell was broken, and even though we returned to Boulder the following year, and spent the next seven there, in Denver, and in places around and in between, something had been lost. 2005 was also the year I began working toward the PhD that, for better and worse, ingrained certain habits of personality or mind, a fact I'm reminded of each time I send a certain older friend an essay to read and he comes back with a cry, always gracefully put, of *too cerebral!* It's a charge other friends have leveled at me as well, arguing that I'm too absent in my writing, that I'm still trying to prove something, and that this keeps them from seeing me in my writing the way they see me in person.

Colorado, in short, is a place I have not been able to shake, and the fact that it's shaped like a box suggests that living and learning here made my thinking too geometrical, as tidy as the state's four borders. To be fair, this may have nothing to do with geography, and maybe it's better to say that living here turned me, regardless of the particulars of *here*, into someone who had forgotten or become disconnected from those deeper, more beguiling sources of human intelligence, someone unmoved by his son's tears or wife's touch, a person incapable of faith, unable to trust others, unwilling, indeed, to trust much of anything, even himself. Someone for whom love and intuition and sex meant nearly nothing, when of course, as I'm coming to see, they mean nearly everything.


After lunch I leave behind the rectilinear highways that quilt the Front Range and begin to follow the winding road, not unlike the river it shadows, leading up the Poudre Canyon. The afternoon blankets the cliffs with strange patterns of light and shadow, and I find myself pulling off and putting on my sunglasses as I bob and weave in the sun. Maybe it's this shifting sense of focus that leads me to consider the trip from another angle: at what point does the tragedy of my self-seriousness turn into comedy, or farce? Those tears in the parking lot: could they not, turned at an even a small angle, become laughable? Maybe not in and of themselves—my catharsis was real—but in the context of my overthinking. What was I crying over, anyway? He's only six, my wife had texted. Lighten up.

Maybe most men face the same struggle, most American men anyway, raised as we are to suffer—and, to the extent it's possible, to heal—in silence, to be the rugged individualists (self-possessed, autonomous) who forge their own paths. I've spent much of my life unconsciously in thrall to these stupid myths about masculinity, or in brief moments like these, bucking them full force, ironically from a secluded canyon halfway between nothing and nowhere. I can't deny that the world looks monstrous to me, that, to paraphrase Paul Auster, it seems to offer no hope of a future. But then I remember my son, a world away, and realize I can't think like that. There is this responsibility for a young life, Auster writes, and in that he has brought this life into being, he must not despair. Minute by minute, hour by hour, as he remains in the presence of his son, attending to his needs, giving himself to this young life, which is a continual injunction to remain in the present, he feels his despair evaporate. And even though he continues to despair, he does not allow himself to despair.

Soon I'm typing in the cabin I first visited years before, or rather in a cabin directly across a gravel path from that cabin. Nothing has changed. All the musty furnishings, right down to the kitchen utensils, have the sheen of other people's lives, but also that mass-manufactured cheapness, which complements the fake-pine paneling lining the walls. The plants are plastic, the paintings pastoral, the decorative pillows embroidered with moose and bears and the words *Cabin Sweet Cabin*. It's as though someone's grandmother decorated the place, but twenty years ago, when it all might have felt crisp and new and not, as it does now, rather sad.

I walk down to the river as the light fades, passing a tree with deep claw marks that could only have been made by a bear, and for a moment I feel more helpless than I probably should, given the nearness of the highway, empty though it is. Solitude can do that to a person, make the bears seem closer than their tracks, the wolves nearer than their howls.

The river is mostly frozen at this altitude, and if I were just a little braver than I am I might walk out to the narrow ripple of open water inexorably running downhill. Before long it's dark enough for stars, and looking up at them from the fake cabin's porch, I'm not at all sure that time is on my side. I can still see the silhouettes of the rocky canyon walls, the dark glow of the horizon, a line of Christmas lights on the proprietor's house at the edge of the property. She's the same brusque woman I remember from all those years before, the one I called Darcy, the same gap in the right corner of her mouth where a tooth should be, the same crappy little store with its rows of chips and condoms and motor oil and beer. Back in the cabin, the cheap clock tacked to the wall keeps ticking.

Begin 45 million years ago with the rise of the Park Range and the Medicine Bow mountains. Begin with the pressure that pushed the rim of the valley up while pulling the center of it down. Begin with the vast, shallow sea that once covered the basin, the shark teeth still lining its ridges. Or begin 12,000 years ago, when the glaciers receded, leaving the lakes and rivers that now form the headwaters of the North Platte. Begin shortly thereafter, when the mountains started to erode, depositing the soil and rocks that constitute the valley floor. Follow the water as it traces its long, meandering path into the Missouri. Follow it farther, to where it meets the Mississippi, just north of what is now St. Louis. Follow it into the Gulf and beyond.

Begin with the Utes and Arapaho, who, prior to the 1820s, used the valley as a hunting ground they called the Bull Pen because it offered no escape. Begin with the fur traders, the coal and gold miners, the logging camps, the ranchers. Begin with the greatest day in Walden history, October 10, 1911, when the trains stopped here for the first time. Begin fifty years later when they stopped for the last. Begin with the coal-seam fire that started south of town in 1915 and which has been burning continuously ever since. Begin with the timber camp in nearby Gould, used to house German prisoners during World War II.

Begin where you like, there's no getting around the truth of Walden. Despite its lovely surroundings, it's as ugly and forlorn a little town as you'll ever find, and driving in this afternoon, having left the cabin for a hotel here late morning, I'm surprised to see the streets largely abandoned and most businesses boarded up. There are more cars propped on blocks, or lining vacant lots, than sitting in driveways, and even the Chamber of Commerce has a *For Sale* sign in its window. It's a derelict place, and the dominant architectural mode is the double-wide, though there are plenty of standard-sized trailers surrounded by chainlink fences as well. My first impulse is to leave as soon as I arrive.

Behind my hotel, aptly named the Antlers Inn for the many taxidermied heads mounted on its walls, there's a drilling rig parked in an empty lot, and when I check in the older woman at the front desk of the lobby-cum-restaurant asks me whether I'm working. It takes me a minute to realize what she means, but when I say I'm not here for that, no, she pulls her long gray-blonde hair into a ponytail and asks whether I'm just playing. It's a better question than she knows.

There's no desk in the room, so I prop myself up on the bed. The view of the mountains is decent, and I can see the sign for the Stockman Bar, alongside of which hangs a banner that reads *Welcome, Hunters!* The bed faces east but if I stand and face west I see the stately courthouse, at once the sturdiest-looking structure in town and, perhaps for that reason, the most out of place. If Walden weren't so depressing, I might say the whole thing is humorous, but as it is the town makes even some of the all-time shitholes of the universe seem luxurious by comparison. I can't think of what people could do here for fun other than drink or smoke pot or cook meth or shoot things. There's so little here you might confuse it for a ghost town. Driving in on Highway 14, I saw enormous ranching operations, thousands of black cattle against the brown brush, but that can't provide a living for everyone, and I seem to be the only tourist passing through. Everyone else is busy snowshoeing or skiing and, well, good for them. May their shiny, water-resistant parkas deter bears.

When I began this book, all those years ago in Prospect, I didn't know that it would eventually lead me here, to the only thriving institution on an otherwise vacant main street. I didn't know that the fantasy of Walden would conclude as reality, though in another way the reverse is equally true: that the dream of self-sufficiency would implode. I suppose I've come because it's always been the first-person speaking, even if I've mostly wrestled against that fact, having been trained to speak from a disembodied place, an objective location somewhere simultaneously out in the ether and trapped behind the eyes. One morning I woke up and thought, *I have to go to Walden, where I've never been.* And now I'm standing next to an old school bus converted into a home, wood burner going full blast, watching the sunset over the Park Range. And now I'm walking the abandoned streets at the edge of town in the dark, lit only by the full moon, under unequivocal skies that stretch as far as the mountains and clouds will let them. Out in the sagebrush I'm feeling some brief piece of what the Utes and Arapaho must have on their summer hunting expeditions: at once the smallness of human life and its integrality, the sense that one might drift across this land, as a seed does, or an elk.

I climb the stairs again, past the antlers, and return to typing on the bed, recording my impressions, but for what? The story isn't here anymore, it's back in Pennsylvania, with my wife and son. I turn on the TV: it's *Star Trek: The Next Generation.* Deanna Troi and a member of a telepathic race, the Cairn, are deep in discussion. The Cairn man, Maques—father of Hedril, played by a young Kirsten Dunst—tells Troi that his people hold nothing back. For our part we value honesty, Troi says, but also privacy. In another scene, Troi quotes Milton, but then has to explain what a poem is, as though it were the fundamental human thing, sitting astride the border between reticence and disclosure. Maques is understandably frustrated by the poem, and by language in general. He often stumbles with words, feels he can't find the right ones, and meanwhile I'm here in my room, drinking beer, considering the light of the Stockman Bar, thinking that, although I haven't had cable for more than a decade, this dialogue would be almost unimaginable on TV today.

I grow hungrier as I watch Troi trying to connect with her mother, who is unconscious on the starship *Enterprise*. She's searching frantically through her mother's repressed memories, aided by the telepathic Cairn, but what's significant to me, sitting on my rented bed in Walden, is that the daughter must save the mother from herself, must redeem her past, though soon the episode is ending and I'm now ravenous, ready to eat whatever the Antlers can offer me, a vegetarian in a ranching town, and as I descend the stairs to the restaurant, I have the thought that maybe I've come here as much to redeem all this estrangement as to make the fantasy real, but I also acknowledge, as I settle into my booth, that this may be the beer talking.

Just as quickly as I arrived in Walden, I am leaving it, under cover of darkness, speeding south down Highway 125 through the broad valley blanketed in sage, toward US 40. There have been no surprises here, except maybe the lack of surprises. And yet for all my sense of anticlimax, I can see how in Walden I perhaps crossed to the other side of some divide, or began to, that the insularity that has defined much of my life must now, with any luck, come to an end. I can't say what's caused or causing this change, but then that's just the point: I can feel it.

The valley is still lit by the full moon and the early predawn light over the mountains to the east. The whole basin is aglow, but it's just me out here on the highway, passing through thousands of black cattle huddled in the cold. Mick Jagger is again, maybe always, on the radio, this time shouting *you're so cold* over and over. I cross the continental divide at Willow Creek Pass just as the sun is emerging, but I don't see another car for some time, not until I'm right outside Granby. By then I'm on the tourist trail, going through ski towns, and every car has something strapped to the roof. I'm climbing up, up into the clouds, and I am so cold, I think, Jagger's right again, he's singing just for me, and then I'm sailing down the mountains, back down through the clouds, at what feels like vertiginous speed. Gravity is carrying me toward Denver, and it feels better than anything I've felt in years to career down the mountain, compelled by different forces than the ones that drew me here.

What if life is about something else? What if you spent it pursuing one thing, only to realize, at the end, you might as easily have focused on another? Such is the deathbed revelation of the central character in my friend Chris's first novel, and it's what I'm thinking as I finally tumble out of the mountains and into the plains, off the interstate and onto US 6. I've left Walden early to visit other friends in Denver, both of whom have new children I haven't met—friends from that time in Boulder when we were first trying to be writers. Now, at thirty-five, one is in med school and, at thirty-six, the other is finishing his PhD. I contacted them last-minute, as I wasn't sure, until I got to Walden, that I would have time to see them, that I would get done what needed doing.

We agreed on 10:30 at a place called Sugar Bake Shop, midway between their two houses, but I reach the city early and head to Jesse's in advance of our rendezvous. He greets me with a cup of coffee, an eight-month-old he keeps calling Birdy (her name is Wren), and one of the best-natured dogs I've ever met, his big black lab Hank. They're living in a part of Engelwood I've never been to, south of the city and just west of the Platte. He's curious about what I've been doing in the mountains, so I describe my modular cabin, the abandoned Poudre Canyon, the privations of Walden. I'm holding Wren as we talk, delighted by her delight in shaking her dad's keys. Meanwhile, he's standing at the counter, washing her bottles. She's a happy baby who looks at me skeptically every now and then, as though she can't quite figure out who I am, what I'm doing here, why I insist on bouncing up and down with her. I see a theme here, I say. Abnegation, self-denial. There's no reason to go to Walden, I add, which is part of the reason I went. Wren moves on from the keys to a plastic teething ring. She's learned the game of throwing something to the floor to make her parents pick it up. Fatherhood suits him, I say. It's hard work, he counters. The hardest, we agree. But it also goes quickly, I say, and then I tell him about my trip to Prospect, the nostalgia I felt there. I didn't cherish it enough, by which I mean, though I don't say this aloud, don't make the same mistake.

Soon it's time for Sugar, but there's the question of the car seat, the football game that afternoon, my flight. We'll drive separately, he says, so I head north up Santa Fe, peeling off, via Mississippi, onto South Broadway, then onto Lincoln, north to 3rd Avenue, then back west one block to Broadway. I can't quite process the change, either in the city or my friend. Vast old industrial sites are now bustling neighborhoods full of the so-called loft-style apartments that were already an epidemic when we left, back in 2012. Denver, like a lot of desert metropolises before it—Phoenix, Las Vegas, LA—is booming. My friend, for his part, is thriving.

As are Rich, his wife Rohini, and their year-old son Arjun, who arrive at Sugar shortly after I do. It's good to see these people, feel their familiar warmth, amplified by these new additions. Everyone has that slightly exhausted look new or newish parents have, with its charming aura. Arjun is full of life, energy, noise. His dad breaks him off bites of cheese, then pieces of quiche. Med school is hard, Rich says, but it's nothing compared to parenting. There's no let-up now, very few moments when I'm home that I'm not meeting his demands. The other med students are twenty-three, some of them. They study eleven hours a day. I'm lucky to study eleven hours a week, he says, memorizing endless catalogues of veins. Jesse arrives with Wren, and it's four adults now, two children, gathered around the table. We're absorbed in the little ones—Jesse's giving Wren a bottle, I'm holding Arjun, trying to keep him happy with a small, squishy truck—and snacking on the homemade pop-tarts that are, I gather, Sugar's specialty. I'm feeling sorry I haven't arranged to spend more time with them, but I needed the other encounter for this one to happen. I don't know how to make that clear, but then it's almost beside the point—almost.


For the rest of the afternoon, after Rohini has taken Arjun home for a nap and Jesse and Rich have taken Wren downtown, where they'll leave her with her mother, Jen, I keep thinking, keep asking myself that question from my friend Chris's novel, what if life is about something else? What if it's about these people I've just eaten homemade pop-tarts with, the children I've just bounced on my lap? What if I've been wrong all these years to put my writing above everything else, above even my family, if that is in fact what I've done? The line of thought feels too easy to be true. But as I'm sitting on the shuttle bus, having said goodbye to the silver Chevy, I start to think that maybe truth isn't so hard, that it's me who's made it that way. Or maybe it's just so bound up in the messy business of living and loving that it's hard to separate it out and to see it for what it is. Maybe, I think, as the bus pulls up to the terminal, that's what I was in Walden to do, separate truth from living. Maybe I've left the former, or my obsession with it, back in Walden and am now free to pursue the latter.

The security line, the train to the concourse, even the wait for the plane pass quickly, although they take nearly two hours. Maybe it's a lingering effect of the altitude, but I'm feeling light enough to float, a buoyancy I'd almost call joy. When I'm actually flying and the beverage cart comes, the woman next to me asks, having stolen a few glances at my screen, whether I'm a writer, and from there we're off and running for the rest of the flight, sharing our lives with one another. She's now a stay-at-home mother of four boys, but she regales me with stories about her career in publishing, her tragicomic Peace Corps service in Senegal, the book she wants to write about it someday. I'm not missing the time going by, but I'm also thinking she's in the story now, that's how it works. And though her trip, like mine, was for her sanity, she's eager to return home, to feel the warmth of those dear to her, even as she knows the feeling won't last more than a few hours, maybe not even more than a few minutes, even though she knows the feeling might dissolve the moment she walks through the door.

And then our plane is landing in Chicago. She's catching a connection to Appleton, I'm catching one to Harrisburg. And I'm saying *I* a lot now, almost stuttering it—*I, I, I, I, I*—and we're in the jetway walking toward the concourse, and I'm remembering how on the plane she said she was leading a mediocre life and I thought that wasn't true at all, that everyone has a story, dozens of stories, and that hers were even better than most. We spill out at gate B4, along with a hundred-some others. You're that way, she says, I'm this way, already turning in the opposite direction. And then, with a smile, goodbye, take care. And I'm thinking as I walk that I hope I don't miss my connection, that I'm also eager, for once, to get home, that I'm headed toward my family, she's headed toward hers, even if we still have a long way to travel, even if neither of us is there just yet.

# | NOTE ON THE TEXT |

This book should not be read as a memoir, strictly speaking, but that isn't to say it should be read as a work of fiction. That it is to be read as *a work of prose* doesn't mean one should approach it as one might the functional and evolutionary insights gathered from the crystalline structure of rubella virus protein E1. The lively debates, recent and otherwise, around the ethics of fact and factitiousness have no or very little place in these pages, which, at the risk of sounding redundant—or worse, tautological—are the records, most of all, of themselves. Insomuch as it is a real invention (as opposed to a fake forgery), the book is, to paraphrase Michael Ondaatje, less a history than a gesture; in it, as in his *Running in the Family*, a well-told lie is (often) worth a thousand facts.

Throughout *Estranger,* I have quoted from other texts, sometimes explicitly, sometimes not, but at no point have I resorted to punctuation as a means of setting these voices off. It is essential to what this book attempts that its narrative voice merges with others, and as indefensible as this lack of formal attribution may be from one perspective, I have sought to keep the book's fluidity intact rather than suffer the straitjacket a stricter regimen would require. Suffice it to say that no book is an island, and this one is in conversation with many others, some of which I've named. Of those I haven't, here is a partial list, for the curious reader: Giorgio Agamben, *The Open*; Paul Auster, *The Invention of Solitude*; Julio Cortázar, *Around the Day in Eighty Worlds*; Annie Dillard, *Teaching a Stone to Talk*; Emmanuel Levinas, *Otherwise Than Being*; Lynn Margulis and Dorion Sagan, *Microcosmos* and *What is Life?*; Christopher Narozny, *Jonah Man*; George Oppen, *Of Being Numerous*; Georges Perec, *Species of Spaces and Other Pieces*; Roger Rosenblatt, *Unless it Moves the Human Heart*; Lynne Sharon Schwartz (ed.), *The Emergence of Memory: Conversations with W.G. Sebald*; Chris Van Allsburg, *The Stranger*; Eliot Weinberger, *An Elemental Thing*; and E.O. Wilson, *The Future of Life*.

Portions of this work have previously appeared (in different form) in *Bombay Gin, Necessary Fiction, Slack Lust,* and *Witness,* and I'm grateful to the editors who shepherded the pieces into print. Over the years I've worked on this book, too many people have contributed to it, directly and indirectly, to name them all, but I need to acknowledge a few people here: Ashraf Ahmed, Sam Bowser, J'Lyn Chapman, Clark Davis, Richard Froude, Laird Hunt, Bhanu Kapil, Jesse Morse, Eleni Sikelianos, Xiaofei Tian, and my dear colleagues in the English Department at Franklin & Marshall College. I'm grateful for the wisdom and friendship of Chris Narozny and Nick Montemarano, without whose keen eyes and close readings this book would not have been possible. I owe an especial debt of gratitude to Zach Savich, Hilary Plum, and Caryl Pagel, for their patience and generosity and vision, for believing in this book and continuously making it better. Finally, an error on my part meant the dedication was omitted from my first book, and considering the vital role my wife has played in my writing and life (if that distinction still makes any sense), it only seems right to end this one by including it here, with love and gratitude: *To Susan, all ways.*

Erik Anderson is the author of *The Poetics of Trespass* (Otis Books/ Seismicity Editions, 2010) and *Flutter Point* (Zone 3 Press, 2017). He teaches creative writing at Franklin & Marshall College, where he also directs the annual Emerging Writers Festival.

**OPEN PROSE SERIES**

*edited by Hilary Plum and Zach Savich*

Anne Germanacos, *Tribute* (2014)
Christian TeBordo, *Toughlahoma* (2015)
Erik Anderson, *Estranger* (2016)

rescuepress.co

RESCUE PRESS